Why
Tragedy
Happens
To Christians

Why
Tragedy
Happens
To Christians

by

Charles Capps

**HARRISON
HOUSE**
P. O. Box 35035
Tulsa, Oklahoma 74135

Library of Congress Catalog Card Number: 80-82992
ISBN 0-89274-175-9
Printed in the United States of America

Contents

Introduction

This book is not intended to be the total answer to the question of tragedy in Christian lives. It is a scriptural help to understanding some unanswered questions in the minds of many.

There are some questions that only God can answer. Some may not fall into any of the categories referred to in this book, but many will.

It is not meant to condemn or belittle anyone, but to help you avoid the things that would bring tragedy to your life.

The Apostle Paul put it this way:

And the servant of the Lord must not strive; but be gentle unto all men, apt to teach, patient,

In meekness instructing those that oppose themselves; if God peradventure will give them repentance to the acknowledging of the truth;

And that they may recover themselves out of the snare of the devil, who are taken captive by him at his will.

2 Timothy 2:24-26

1

The Destroyer

It was late afternoon. Birds were singing; kids were playing. Suddenly, the serenity was broken by the sound of squeeling tires and a loud crash. There was silence for a few minutes, then the familiar sound of sirens filled the air.

Tragedy had struck! Two people were dead; others were injured.

As people gathered around, doing what they could to help, bits of conversation could be heard:

"Isn't that Brother and Sister So-and-so? I just talked with him yester-day."

"They were such good people. What a tragedy!"

Then the inevitable question is asked — a question that will be asked many times, before and after the funeral:

"Why did this happen to them? They were such good Christians!"

It is best not to try to answer such a question. The answer could be harder to believe than the accident itself. In this life, no one may ever know the true answer for sure.

Most people try desperately to help God out of what appears to be a bad situation by giving their own opinions, based on their religious ideas.

They very often come up with such statements as: "Well, God knows best. You know what the Bible says, *All things work together for good to those that love God.*"

This is too often the case, and God is left looking like a killer. Small children grow up believing that God is responsible for such tragedies.

What does the Bible really say?

Is God the destroyer?

Is God a killer?

In answering this, the words of Jesus ring very clear: *The thief cometh not but for to steal, and to kill, and to destroy: I am come that they might have life and have it more abundantly* (John 10:10).

The Greek word translated *destroyer* means "ruiner; specifically, a venomous serpent."

Satan is the destroyer!

In such tragedies, it might be years later before some important information comes to light. No one mentioned it at the time because they thought it unimportant; but a distant relative casually mentions that he remembers hearing them say *they prayed that they would die together.*

This then raises another question: *Did God answer that prayer; or did they open the door to the destroyer?*

The Need for Knowledge

John Osteen made a statement that I will never forget. He said, "God's people don't need so much *inspiration* as they need *information.*" What a profound statement for the day in which we live!

In Hosea 4:6, God said, *My people are destroyed for lack of knowledge: because thou hast rejected knowledge, I will also reject thee, that thou shalt be no priest to me: seeing thou hast forgotten the law of thy God, I will also forget thy children.*

Here God reveals **the major source of destruction:** *My people are destroyed for lack of knowledge.*

A person cannot believe any further than he has knowledge. He can have great zeal; but without knowledge to go with it, his zeal will be misdirected.

Lack of knowledge is probably the number one reason tragedy comes to many Christians. This lack of knowledge causes people to fall into needless problems, troubles, suffering, sickness, and destruction.

Second Peter 1:2 tells us that *grace and peace* are *multiplied* unto us *through the knowledge of God and of Jesus our Lord.*

Grace is God's willingness to use His power and His ability on your behalf, even though you do not deserve it. According to this verse, *God's willingness* is multiplied to an individual as he gains *the knowledge of God*.

Verse 3 says, . . . *According as his divine power hath given unto us all things that pertain unto life and godliness, through the knowledge of him that hath called us to glory and virtue.*

All things that pertain to life and godliness are *already* ours; but in order to enter into these things that pertain to life, we must have knowledge of it.

. . . *Whereby are given unto us exceeding great and precious promises: that by these ye might be partakers of the divine nature* (v. 4).

It is by *the divine promises* that we are made partakers of *the divine nature of God*.

Again, verse 3 says, *His divine power hath given unto us all things that pertain unto life and godliness.* It is God's divine power that gives us these things. How? Through the knowledge of God.

These things come by knowing, believing, and acting on these promises. Then you partake of God's divine provision.

Know it. Believe it. Act on it. Receive it. God has offered it to you; but if you don't know that, you will not enter into it. You may believe the lies of satan and fall into needless problems, hurt, harm, and trouble.

Without the knowledge of God, you will believe the things you have heard through religious circles: that God sometimes sends tragedy to teach you and make you stronger. This will seem right to you, but it is not right. It is not what God's Word says.

Someone has made the statement: "The devil is no more than an unwilling servant of God." In other words, the devil is performing God's work, causing people to grow stronger by tempting, testing, and trying them.

That same individual said, "God never did promise to deliver us out of troubles. He always sends troubles to make us stronger and more like Jesus."

This kind of thinking sounds good to the religious mind, but it is a lie of the devil!

Psalm 91 brings light to this subject.

A thousand shall fall at thy side, and ten thousand at thy right hand; but it shall not come nigh thee.

Only with thine eyes shalt thou behold and see the reward of the wicked.

Because thou hast made the Lord, which is my refuge, even the most high, thy habitation;

There shall no evil befall thee, neither shall any plague come nigh thy dwelling (vv. 7-10).

Some people do not know that *God is their habitation,* that *God is the deliverer.*

The individuals who believe that the devil is doing God a service are opening the door to tragedy and inviting satan into their lives. There is no defense for them.

They reason this way: *If satan is doing it for God, then who am I to resist God?*

But, satan is **not** doing it for God; he is doing it to destroy God's creation. He is an enemy of God and man.

There shall no evil befall thee, neither shall any plague come nigh thy dwelling.

For he shall give his angels charge over thee, to keep thee in all thy ways.

They shall bear thee up in their hands, lest thou dash thy foot against a stone.

Thou shalt tread upon the lion and adder: the young lion and the dragon shalt thou trample under feet.

Because he hath set his love upon me, therefore will I deliver him: and I will set him on high, because he hath known my name.

He shall call upon me, and I will answer him: I will be with him in trouble; I will deliver him, and honour him.

With long life will I satisfy him, and shew him my salvation.

Psalm 91:10-16

Certainly, God said He would deliver us out of trouble. That is **the will, the purpose, and the plan of God for our lives.**

Speaking of Jesus, Galatians 1:4 says, *Who gave himself for our sins, that he might deliver us from this present evil world, according to the will of God and our Father.*

In other words, **it is the will of God that we be delivered from this present evil world,** or the evil that is in the world. It is **not** God's will for us to go through all the evil — problems, tests, trials, troubles, tribulations — that the devil has to offer.

We have heard many sermons about how God led the children of Israel in the wilderness; and most of these sermons seem to convey that the "wilderness experience" was to perfect them or make them stronger.

But it **did not** make them stronger. It **did not** perfect their faith. It **was not** the will of God that they be in the wilderness all those years.

Their "wilderness experience" was not God's blessing — it was a curse!

It was not designed to make the children of Israel stronger. It was designed to kill them — and it killed all those over twenty years of age. The "wilderness experience" killed the doubters.

The knowledge of why Israel was in the wilderness will give you a different perspective of God.

Wisdom — Ability to Apply Knowledge

Knowledge is vitally important, but knowledge alone is not the answer. It must be combined with wisdom. **Wisdom is the ability to use knowledge.** Knowledge without the wisdom to apply it is inadequate for any situation.

Wisdom crieth without; she uttereth her voice in the streets:

She crieth in the chief place of concourse, in the openings of the gates: in the city she uttereth her words, saying,

How long, ye simple ones, will ye love simplicity? and the scorners delight in their scorning, and fools hate knowledge?

Turn you at my reproof: behold, I will pour out my spirit unto you, I will make known my words unto you.

Because I have called, and ye refused; I have stretched out my hand, and no man regarded;

But ye have set at nought all my counsel, and would none of my reproof: I also will laugh at your calamity; I will mock when your fear cometh;

When your fear cometh as desolation, and your destruction cometh as a whirlwind; when distress and anguish cometh upon you.

Then shall they call upon me, but I will not answer; they shall seek me early, but they shall not find me:

For that they hated knowledge, and did not choose the fear of the Lord.

They would none of my counsel: they despised all my reproof.

Therefore shall they eat of the fruit of their own way, and be filled with their own devices.

Proverbs 1:20-31

This is where many Christians miss it. When problems come and calamity strikes, they seek for wisdom, but do not find it.

Why?

Because **fear** has come. **Fear will stop the flow of God's wisdom.**

For the turning away of the simple shall slay them, and the prosperity of fools shall destroy them.

But whoso hearkeneth unto me shall dwell safely, and shall be quiet from fear of evil (vv. 32,33).

Whoso hearkeneth to the wisdom of God. That person shall dwell safely and be quiet from fear of evil.

The force of fear can stop God's wisdom from coming and keep faith from working.

Jesus, speaking of the end-times, said: . . . *Men's hearts failing them for fear, and for looking after those things which are coming on the earth* . . . (Luke 21:26).

Many may say, "Yes, that has already come to pass because many people are having heart attacks."

There could be a double meaning to this; but if you search the Scriptures, you will find that Jesus never talked about the physical heart of a man. He talked about the heart as being the spirit of man, the inner man. In other words, your human spirit can fail because of fear.

The spirit of man is designed to produce or bring you to the very thing that you speak out of your mouth. It is designed to bring into manifestation the things you desire. It is the soil of the kingdom within you.

Jesus was speaking to the scribes and Pharisees when He said:

> *Oh generation of vipers, how can ye, being evil, speak good things? for out of the abundance of the heart the mouth speaketh.*
>
> *A good man out of the good treasure of the heart bringeth forth good things: and an evil man out of the evil treasure bringeth forth evil things.*
>
> Matthew 12:34-36

A good man out of the good treasure of his heart (his spirit) brings forth good things. He cannot bring forth good if there is no good planted in his heart, for everything produces after its kind.

Evil Report

The scribes and Pharisees had evil in their hearts. You cannot bring forth good when there is evil in your heart. Now, don't equate evil only with being wicked. There are many Christians who have things in their hearts which God considers to be evil.

If you want to know what God considers evil, look at the 13th chapter of Numbers. This was God's people and He had promised them the land. It belonged to them. It was theirs. But they would not go in and possess it.

They heard the Word of the Lord, but refused to believe it. Twelve men were sent to spy out the land. Ten brought back what God called "an evil report."

They reported what they *saw,* what they *felt,* and what they *heard.* God called that "an evil report."

Some might question: *Is everything we see, feel, and hear an evil report?*

No, certainly not! It is only an **evil report** when it **disagrees with God's Word.**

God said to His people, "I have given you the land. Go in and possess it."

But they returned and said, "We are not able. We can't do it. There are

giants over there. We are like grass-
hoppers in their sight, and so were we
in our own eyes.''

They had *grasshopper vision*. They
also had a bad case of the *what if's:*
"but *what if* God doesn't see us
through?''

Maybe you have had the same
problem. Remember: God calls that
kind of report "evil."

When you relate that to what Jesus
said in the 12th chapter of Matthew,
you realize that He was not only talking
about the scribes and Pharisees, He was
also talking about an individual who
has in his heart things that are contrary
to what God has spoken. When that
person opens his mouth, those things
will come out.

Jesus said, *A good man out of the
good treasure of his heart. . . .* The
Greek shows that the word *treasure* is
the same word we use for "deposit."
So, a good man out of the good *deposit*
of his heart brings forth good things.

What have you been depositing in your heart?

If it is contrary to God's Word, then God considers it evil. If you speak it often enough, it will become a part of you. It will bring forth the very thing that is in your heart.

Some people do not understand this. They say, "Why in the world do these 'faith' people always talk victory, always calling things that are not as though they were?"

The answer is simple: **We are applying the principles of God's wisdom.**

Imitate God

In Ephesians 5:1, *The Amplified Bible* says, "Therefore be imitators of God — copy Him and follow His example — as well-beloved children imitate their father."

If you are going to *imitate God,* you have to *talk like Him*.

Get in agreement with God. Then you will call things that are not as though they were until they are!

Exposed to the Answers

Some people say, "Now, Brother, that is just ignoring the problem. That is like an ostrich, just sticking his head in the sand."

No, we are not ignoring the problem; we are doing something about it. We are applying the principles of God's Word and using the wisdom of God.

God's wisdom is above man's wisdom. Man likes to continually talk about his problems, and his words paint the image of that problem within him.

Continue to talk it and it will be fully developed inside you. **Your words build the image.**

Let me give you an example. Suppose you decided to take a picture of a group of people, but you focused the camera toward yourself and snapped the picture. How many people from that group would be in the picture?

None, of course!

Why?

Because you exposed the film to the wrong object. You had the camera turned the wrong way!

The spirit of man is designed to produce the very thing that is imaged in it. Like the film of a camera, it will bring forth the exact thing to which it has been exposed. If you expose it to the problem, you cannot expect to receive the answer.

Good or Evil Is Your Choice

Allow me to paraphrase something Jesus said: "A good man out of the good deposit of his heart brings forth what his heart has been exposed to, either good or bad. *The choice is yours.*"

Someone might say, "I don't understand why God made it that way."

God *didn't* make it that way. Adam *chose* that way in the Garden of Eden when he chose to eat the fruit of the tree of knowledge of good and evil. *The Amplified Bible* calls it "the tree of the knowledge of blessing and calamity."

Adam *chose* calamity in the Garden. It was not God's will.

Quite often, people who do not understand this say, "God allowed it to happen." If you believe God allowed it, you will be inviting calamity into your life. This is the deception of satan.

Paul tells us in 2 Corinthians 11:3, *But I fear, lest by any means, as the serpent beguiled Eve through his subtilty, so your minds should be corrupted from the simplicity that is in Christ.*

He did not say a thing about satan being so powerful and so almighty that he would run over you and destroy you. He said, "I am afraid he will *deceive* you."

Satan is the destroyer, but his power is limited to deception. He deceives people into believing the wrong thing. He deceives them into using their own authority and their own words against themselves to bring about the disaster he has planned for them.

If you get a *Strong's Concordance* and look up the words *devil, satan,* and *deceiver,* you will discover what power is attributed to him. You will be amazed at how little power he actually has. The most powerful thing satan has working for him is *deception*.

To survive in the earth, we must have the wisdom and knowledge of God. God's people are destroyed for lack of knowledge, but *the Lord giveth wisdom: out of his mouth cometh knowledge and understanding* (Prov. 2:6).

2

The Tree of Life or Death

God provided a tree of life in the Garden of Eden. Man could choose life or death. Satan wanted to tap the tree of life. He was going after it when he tempted Eve to sin.

Someone may ask, "Why didn't he just pull the fruit and eat?"

He couldn't do that. He had no body. He had to borrow the body of a serpent to talk to Eve. He had to get Adam to eat of the tree of life; then if everything worked as planned, he could tap into the tree *through man*. That is the only way satan could get to the tree of life.

But, thank God, it didn't work the way he planned! God is smarter than the devil. God put man out of the Garden before he could eat of the tree of life. The tree of life would have made man immortal. Had he eaten after he committed high treason, he would have been an immortal sinner.

Proverbs 15:4 tells us: *A wholesome tongue is a tree of life.* You can see that the fruit poisoned Adam's tongue and it became an unruly evil.

The *King James Version* calls the tree, "the tree of the knowledge of good and evil." But *The Amplified Bible* says, "of blessing and calamity."

Calamity means "hurt, harm, trouble." Everything that is bad! Adam certainly did not need calamity, but he chose it in the Garden.

Adam Had Dominion

Adam was created to be god of this world.

And God said, Let us make man in our image, after our likeness: and let them have dominion over the fish of the sea, and over the fowl of the air, and over the cattle, and over all the earth, and over every creeping thing that creepeth upon the earth.

So God created man in his own image, in the image of God created he him; male and female created he them.

Genesis 1:26,27

The original Hebrew word *likeness* meant "an exact duplication in kind." God is a spirit and man was created in the likeness of God. Therefore, man is a spirit being; he has a soul; and he lives in a body. Man is capable of operating on the same level of faith as God. Jesus said, *All things are possible to him that believeth* (Mark 9:23).

It is true that man fell; but the reborn human spirit has been raised to God's level of faith. That does not mean you are able to create worlds, but you are capable of changing the one you live in.

Jesus said to the disciples in Matthew 17:20, . . . *If ye have faith as a grain of mustard seed, ye shall say unto this mountain, Remove hence to yonder place; and it shall remove; and nothing shall be impossible unto you.*

Nothing shall be impossible to you. *Nothing!*

But God gave man a choice. He has always done that. He gave the angels a choice. They did not have the *right* to choose, but they made a choice. They did not have the right to choose their words; they were to speak only what God said.

But the Anointed Cherub (now the devil) said, *I will exalt my throne* (Is. 14:13; Ezek. 28:14). He did not have a right to say that. He was a created being. But he made that choice and he broke rank with God.

Man's Right

In the Garden, **man had a right to choose his words.** God always gives a choice. He gave Adam the right to choose. Man made the choice and he chose calamity.

God has now made restoration available to man by the rebirth of the human spirit. *Whatsoever is born of God overcometh the world* (1 John 5:4).

The reborn human spirit is capable of operating on the same level of faith with God. You can believe things in your heart that you cannot believe with your head. But whatever you expose your spirit to is what will show up. The words you speak will produce after their kind.

If there is fear in your heart, it will come out in words and produce more fear.

If there is faith in your heart, it will come out in words and produce more faith.

Like a snowball going down a hill, it will get larger and stronger the further it goes. Your words either build or destroy.

No person would take a camera, focus it on the problem, and expect to get a picture of the answer. Yet, satan has deceived the Body of Christ into praying the problem and speaking things they do not desire, until it creates an image of the problem on the film of their spirits.

As they meditate on them, these fear images become clear. They perfect that image by thought, meditation, and words. Then they believe more in the troubles and calamities than in God's ability to put them over or deliver them. **This opens the door to satan and gives him his foothold.**

Satan is out to tap **your** tree of life. *The wholesome tongue is that tree of life.*

Fear Is Destruction

> *But whoso hearkeneth unto me shall dwell safely, and shall be quiet from fear of evil.*
>
> Proverbs 1:33

Let's look at something Job said in the light of this scripture.

> *For the thing which I greatly feared is come upon me, and that which I was afraid of is come unto me. I was not in safety, neither had I rest, neither was I quiet; yet trouble came.*
>
> Job 3:25,26

Isn't that amazing? When the principles of fear, defeat, and disaster were set in motion, they produced that very thing. Job did more than just fear

— he *greatly* feared. He was highly developed in his fears.

Learn to resist fear like you resist the devil himself!

Fear is a design of satan to destroy you.

Fear is not of God. *For God hath not given us the spirit of fear; but of power, and of love, and of a sound mind* (2 Tim. 1:7).

God said, "Whoever hearkens to Me shall dwell safely and *be quiet* from fear of evil."

But Job said, "I was not in safety."

The very indictment satan brought against God was, "You hedged him about on every side; I couldn't get to him." (Job 1:10.)

But Job said he was not in safety. He was afraid. He was fearful. He was highly developed in his fear.

I have a wall plaque, given to me by my daughter, which says, *Fear knocked at the door. Faith answered and there was no one there.*

Every time fear knocks, if faith answers, there will be no one there!

Both faith and fear are transmitted by words. Speak faith and you will have faith. Speak fear and you will have fear. **Words transmit fear or faith. The choice is yours.**

Authority of Words

Proverbs 4:20,21 says, *My son, attend to my words; incline thine ear unto my sayings. Let them not depart from thine eyes; keep them in the midst of thine heart.*

This has a two-fold meaning: You can see the Word of God with your physical eyes, but this is talking about the eyes of the spirit. Let them not depart from the eye of faith. Keep them in the midst of your heart.

You can do that by speaking the Word, by quoting it aloud. The psalmist David asks, *Lord, who shall dwell in thy holy hill? Then he answers, He that . . . speaketh the truth in his heart* (Ps. 15:1,2).

How did you get the truth into your heart? By speaking it there. The authority of your own spoken words will carry more weight with your human spirit than anyone's words.

Keep them in the midst of thine heart.

Let's notice what God told Joshua.

This book of the law shall not depart out of thy mouth; but thou shalt meditate therein day and night, that thou mayest observe to do according to all that is written therein: for then thou shalt make thy way prosperous, and then thou shalt have good success.

Joshua 1:8

If you want the Word of God in your heart, you must keep it in your mouth.

For they (God's words) *are life unto those that find them, and health to all their flesh. Keep thy heart with all diligence; for out of it are the issues of life.*

Proverbs 4:22,23

One translation says out of the heart flow "the forces of life." When it says *heart,* it is not referring to the blood pump, but to the spirit. Out of the spirit flow the forces of life.

Exposing your heart to the Word of God will absolutely change the direction of your life.

The force of life is in your spirit. That same Spirit that raised Jesus from the dead dwelling in you shall quicken your mortal body. He will make alive your mortal body. (Rom. 8:11.)

Contrary Speech

Put away from thee a froward mouth, and perverse lips put far from thee (Prov. 4:24). *Perverse lips* means "to turn about; deviate from right; corrupt, stubborn, or contrary speech."

Christians are inviting tragedy by the idle words they speak.

Hebrews 4:12,13 says:

For the word of God is quick, and powerful, and sharper than any twoedged sword, piercing even to the dividing asunder of soul and spirit, and of the joints and marrow, and is a discerner of the thoughts and intents of the heart.

Neither is there any creature that is not manifest in his sight: but all things are naked and opened unto the eyes of him with whom we have to do.

Notice it says all things are *naked* and *open* unto His eyes. The Word of God is quick and powerful and sharper than any twoedged sword. That two-edged sword is the tongue that speaks harmful words.

Notice Proverbs 12:18: *There is that speaketh like the piercings of a sword: but the tongue of the wise is health.* People can speak against you, but the Word of God in your mouth will stop their words.

Christians are the most dangerous people on earth with their mouths. Their words are powerful and can bring destruction. Their words are powerful because they come from the reborn human spirit.

If you have a group of Christians talking against you and you do not have the Word of God going out your mouth, you may find yourself in serious problems and not know what is causing it. That is one reason it is so important to keep God's Word in your mouth. The Word of God is quicker, more powerful, and sharper than all that talk against you.

Bridle the Tongue

Let's go to the book of James for some words of wisdom.

> *For in many things we offend all. If any man offend not* (Greek: stumble not) *in word the same is a perfect man, and able also to bridle the whole body.*
>
> *Behold, we put bits in the horses' mouths, that they may obey us; and we turn about their whole body.*
> James 3:2,3

Both verses are talking about the body. He said you can turn a horse in any direction just by putting pressure on his tongue.

> *Behold also the ships, which though they be so great, and are driven of fierce winds, yet are they turned about with a very small helm, whithersoever the governor listeth.*
>
> James 3:4

Notice, he likens the tongue to the rudder of a ship which the captain uses to turn the ship wherever he desires. If you do not like the way things are going in your life, **take control of the rudder** — *the tongue.*

Suppose a big freighter is coming into port in Los Angeles. As it moves slowly toward the dock, the captain yells, "Look! We're going to hit the dock! We're going to hit the dock!"

Finally, someone yells back, "Hey, dummy, turn the rudder!"

That is exactly what is happening to many Christians. They run into a problem and begin to talk the problem. They are setting the rudder — exposing their heart to the problem.

The heart is the governor; it controls the rudder. **The tongue is the rudder.**

It will turn about your whole body for good or for evil. **The governing factor is what you speak into your heart!**

Out of the abundance of the heart the mouth speaketh.

Proverbs 18:7: *A fool's mouth is his destruction, and his lips are the snare of his soul.*

3

The Kindling of Destroying Fire

Even so the tongue is a little member, and boasteth great things. Behold, how great a matter a little fire kindleth!

James 3:5

Behold means "look." Look at what great force a little fire kindles! It starts out small, not amounting to much; but, if not controlled, it can grow into a destructive force.

Perhaps you have a fireplace in your home. Jerry Savelle gives this excellent illustration about kindling:

Have you ever put a log about 18 inches in diameter in the fireplace, then tried to use paper matches to light a fire? It won't work! You have to use kindling — little splinters of wood.

You take one of those paper matches and light one splinter. That splinter will light another one and, before long, you have a fire that will burn the log.

But what has happened to the kindling? It is completely burned and nobody thinks anything about it. No one talks about the kindling. They all want to talk about the fire.

> *Behold, how great a matter a little fire kindleth!*
>
> *And the tongue is a fire, a world of iniquity: so is the tongue among our members, that it defileth the whole body, and setteth on fire the course of nature; and it is set on fire of hell.*
>
> James 3:5,6

God certainly did not set it on fire of hell! *For every good gift and every perfect gift is from above, and cometh down from the Father of lights, with whom is no variableness, neither shadow of turning* (James 1:17).

The Amplified Bible says it sets on fire "the wheel of birth — or cycle of man's nature."

The body was designed to live forever. It was created to perpetuate itself. Every seven to eleven years, each

cell in your body changes. Not one cell
in your body today was there eleven
years ago. Medical science does not
understand why the physical body of
man ages and dies.

Satan introduced death into the
earth through man when Adam ate of
the tree of calamity.

*The tongue setteth on fire the course
of nature and it is set on fire of hell.*
Your tongue can defile the whole
body. How? By exposing the human
spirit (the heart) to problems, troubles,
and wrong thinking.

Satan is out to tap your tree of life.
The wholesome tongue is a tree of life.
When we get to heaven, we will be able
to partake of the original tree of life.
If you read about the tree of life in
Revelation 22:2, you will find that the
leaves are for the healing of the nations.

Do you know what causes all the
wars and troubles on earth? Words!
Words of disagreement, words of strife
— all can be traced back to words.

The tongue defiles the whole body and sets on fire the course of nature. If *used* wrongly, the tongue can stop the natural healing forces in the body; yet, the *wholesome* tongue is a tree of life.

> *For every kind of beasts, and of birds, and of serpents, and of things in the sea, is tamed, and hath been tamed of mankind:*
>
> *But the tongue can no man tame; it is an unruly evil, full of deadly poison.*
>
> James 3:7,8

If you do not control your tongue, you will be inviting tragedy into your life.

At a certain meeting, I heard a man jokingly say, "Well, the way my luck's been running, I'll probably get run over by a freight train before I get home."

He didn't get run over by a freight train, but he said that for a joke. He may say that year after year and nothing happens. But if he continues to speak that way, you may pick up the paper some morning and find that he was run over by the 9:23 freight!

Then everybody wants to know, "Why did God allow that to happen? He was such a godly man."

The kindling was started years before when he jokingly said, "I'll probably get run over by a freight train before I get home." He made foolish jokes like that down through the years. He spoke it until, finally, over a period of years, it became a seed in his spirit that produced death. It did not happen just because he said it once, but he set a law into motion. (Mark 11:23.) Satan tapped his tree of life and used it as a tree of death.

The Human Spirit — A Production Center

The human spirit is designed to produce what is placed within it. Out of the human spirit flow the forces of life:

A good man out of the good deposit of his heart brings forth good things.

An evil man out of the evil deposit brings forth evil things.

When the 9:23 came along, that man was on the track. He felt impressed to go somewhere at that exact time.

The spirit of man is designed to produce what you speak.

> *As in water face answereth to face, so the heart of man to man.*
> Proverbs 27:19

The human spirit is like film in a camera. When you expose the film of a camera to a problem, it will produce the exact image to which it was exposed.

Suppose you had the best car that money could buy. You might say, "I'll take a picture of it and show everyone what a beautiful car I have." But then you find the worst wreck in the junkyard, focus your camera, and snap it.

When you show the picture to a friend, he says, "What in the world is that?"

You tell him, "I don't understand it. I have the best car money can buy.

Why did this photo turn out this way?''

The answer is obvious: **You exposed the film to the wrong object,** so you did not get the results you wanted from the film.

The more you expose your spirit to the problems of life, the more problems you are going to produce.

This is where many people come against the faith message. They say, "That's mind over matter. That's positive thinking."

No. This is as far from positive thinking as East is from West. It is the *positive faith* of God's Word, building upon the principle of applying God's wisdom to man's spirit. It will control your spirit, for out of the abundance of the heart, the mouth speaks. That which is continually spoken out the mouth will eventually come to pass.

> *But the tongue can no man tame; it is an unruly evil, full of deadly poison. Therewith bless we God, even the Father; and therewith curse*

we men, which are made after the similitude of God.

Out of the same mouth proceedeth blessing and cursing. My brethren, these things ought not so to be.

James 3:8-10

These things ought not be so, *but they are!*

Someone said, "It sounds like a hopeless case."

No, thank God, it is not! The tongue *no man* can tame with his *natural* ability. It takes the supernatural ability of God to bridle the tongue.

Seek the Answer

You expose your spirit to the problem through words. I am not saying you should ignore the problem. This is where the faith message comes under fire. People say, "They're just ignoring the problem."

No, we are not *ignoring the problem;* we are just refusing to give the problem ascendancy. We are *disarming the problem* by using God's Word, by speaking the answer.

Keeping the answer in your mouth is the key to solving any problem.

The more you talk the problem, the more you believe in it. The more you believe in it, the more you will talk it. The problem will grow greater within you until it consumes you inside and out. It will destroy you. It is a design of satan to do just that.

God created man so that his spirit (heart) would bring forth the good things of life.

When Adam ate of the tree of knowledge, he chose calamity. His tongue was poisoned. The original Hebrew word for *serpent,* as used in Genesis 3:1, is *poisoner.* The *poisoner* came into the Garden. The *poisoner* poisoned Adam's tongue. When Adam ate the fruit, he gained the ability to produce calamity by the words of his mouth.

Satan did not tell Adam the whole truth. The day he ate of the fruit, Adam lost control of his tongue.

Adam's words would produce good or evil, but he lost control of his words.

Has this situation ever happened to you:

Your wife has gone shopping. You wait for her in the parking lot for an hour. But you determine: "I'm going to be nice to her. I'll just walk in love. I'm not going to say a word."

Then just as soon as she opens the car door, you explode! "Where in the world have you been? I've been sitting out here for three hours!"

You purposed not to do it, but you did it anyway! **It takes the supernatural ability of God to tame the tongue.**

A lady was visiting a friend of ours while my daughter was there. The lady walked through the yard where the children where playing on swings. She said, "All right now, you just watch.

One of you is going to get hurt. Just watch and see!"

As soon as she finished "prophesying," she went into the house. Within five minutes, one of the children came in with his head cut open.

She spoke it, and it came to pass the same hour!

Fear-filled words bring *the devil* on the scene.

Faith-filled words bring *God* on the scene.

Choose Your Words Carefully

God gave us our tongues and the ability to choose our own words to put us over in life. But many are using their tongues and their words to work against them.

Even so the tongue is a little member . . . but how great a matter a little fire kindleth. So many times, people say things, without even realizing what they are saying.

A lady drove my wife and me from the airport to a motel in a certain city.

In the course of conversation, she made this one statement at least five times:

"You know, that just tears my heart out."

I finally said, "I wouldn't say that if I were you."

She looked astonished, not knowing what she had said.

One day I was in a little restaurant in a town near where I live, eating a hamburger. A lady came in and asked the owner, "How is Mrs. So-and-so?"

The owner said she was doing fine; then added, "You know, she had that operation on her foot and she's just tickled to death. She hasn't had any pain since the operation, and she's just tickled to death!"

I sat there thinking, *I wonder what they would think if I said, "Isn't that a shame. She got her foot healed and now she's dead!"*

They would have asked, "What are you talking about?" They probably were not even aware of what came out their mouths.

Suppose you say four or five times a day, "My back is just killing me!" or, "I'll tell you, this thing is going to be the death of me yet!" You have started the kindling burning.

By the time the fire gets going and it comes to pass, everyone will have forgotten about the kindling that started the whole thing. It will have disappeared and people will say, "Why did God allow it to happen?"

He didn't allow it. You invited it! You set it in motion with the words of your mouth. **Satan took advantage of your words.**

It is a law of God that a man will have *whatsoever* he says, if he believes and doubts not in his heart. Jesus said so in Mark 11:23:

> *For verily I say unto you, That whosoever shall say unto this mountain, Be thou removed, and be thou cast into the sea; and shall not doubt in his heart, but shall believe that those things which he saith shall*

come to pass; he shall have whatsoever he saith.

The more you say it, the more you will believe it. The more you believe it, the more you will say it. Eventually, it will come to pass.

While I was teaching on this scripture in a certain city, the Spirit of God said, "I have told My people they can have what they say, but My people are saying what they have!" That is simple, but profound.

You *say* what you *have* and you *have* what you *say*. You *have* what you *say* because you *say* what you *have*. It's a vicious circle!

You will never go beyond the place you are now, nor have more than you have now, unless you say and believe something you do not have.

God's Word in Your Mouth

God designed His Word to work for you.

This is the theme of my book, *God's Creative Power Will Work For You.* At the time of this writing, there are over 600,000 in print. I have received two letters from people who did not like the book at all.

One man said, "It's the most blasphemous thing I have ever read. You must think you're God by saying, 'I'm the righteousness of God, and I overcome evil with good.'"

No, I was only saying what God said about me and every believer, but some people do not understand that.

A lady wrote and said, "You have done the most fantastic job of taking Scriptures out of context that I have ever seen."

But those Scriptures were written to every believer!

Another lady wrote and told me about a tragedy that was averted because she confessed the Word from that little book. She said, "When I received your book, my children and I began to quote the Scriptures every morning and every night."

They confessed: "I'm the Body of Christ. The enemy has no power over me. I overcome evil with good. The Greater One dwells within me. Greater is He that is in me than he that is in the world. In my pathway is life and there is no death."

She wrote, "One day our young child was found floating face down in the swimming pool. He had been confessing each day for weeks: 'In my pathway is life and there is no death.' (Prov. 12:28.)

"He was taken from the pool lifeless. My husband began to press on him and confess the Word of God over him. Life came back into him! Twenty minutes later he was running around playing!"

What do you suppose is going to happen when tragedy comes to the door of those who do not believe these promises?

Many have invited tragedy with their words. The devil will buddy-up with you. He will go home with you, then bring sickness and poverty to your house if you allow him to.

The reason the devil comes to some houses is because he is welcome there. Some people think the devil is doing God a service. Some have actually invited him in. **They have invited tragedy by not knowing the purpose and will of God.**

James 4:7 says, *Submit yourselves therefore to God. Resist the devil, and he will flee from you.* That is the will of God. It is never God's will for you to buddy-up with the devil and invite him home with you.

The devil will stay where there is least resistance. If you think sickness, disease, problems, and troubles are making you stronger and perfecting you, then you will have no resistance to disease and problems.

But if you will walk in the principles of God's Word, keep God's Word in your mouth, and apply what God has said, you can be victorious over these problems of life.

The Book of Proverbs gives you a choice:

> *A fool's mouth is his destruction, and his lips are the snare of his soul.*
>
> Proverbs 18:7

> *The righteous is delivered out of trouble, and the wicked cometh in his stead.*
>
> Proverbs 11:8

Let's look at a prayer that Jesus prayed in John, chapter 17. We would do well to take heed to His words. In verse 15, He says, *I pray not that thou shouldest take them out of the world, but that thou shouldest keep them from the evil.* Jesus is praying that God would keep them from evil.

The word translated *evil* is from a Greek word meaning "calamitous, ill, disease, grievous, hurt, harm." In other words, evil is anything that would be considered bad.

. . . *that thou shouldest keep them from evil.* This must be the will of God, or Jesus would not have prayed it.

When you link this with Matthew 6:10 where Jesus prayed, *Thy kingdom come. Thy will be done in earth, **as it is in heaven,*** then you know this is the will of God for the earth.

Let it be on earth, as it is in heaven, that we be delivered from evil. According to Galatians 1:4, Jesus gave Himself for our sins, that He *might deliver us from this present evil world, according to the will of God our Father.*

You can confess: "No evil will befall me, neither shall any plague come nigh my dwelling. He has given His angels charge over me. My pathway is life; there is no death."

Why? Because these are direct quotes from God's Word.

The name of the Lord is a strong tower: the righteous runneth into it, and is safe.

Proverbs 18:10

The fear of Lord tendeth to life: and he that hath it shall abide satisfied; he shall not be visited with evil.

Proverbs 19:23

4

Those Who Oppose Themselves

Everyone has questioned God at one time or another. Some people even get mad at God. But there is nothing to be gained by getting mad at God.

A lack of knowledge causes you to accept things you thought God sent, when God was not responsible at all. It was the devil that sent them!

The servant of the Lord must not strive; but be gentle unto all men, apt to teach, patient,

In meekness instructing those that oppose themselves; if God peradventure will give them repentance to the acknowledging of the truth;

And that they may recover themselves out of the snare of the devil, who are taken captive by him at his will.

2 Timothy 2:24-26

Notice Paul says, *In meekness instructing those that oppose themselves.* Many Christians today are opposing themselves.

Many people are right in their hearts, but wrong in their heads. They lack the knowledge of God. They have been taught incorrectly and have assumed certain things. Some of their preconceived ideas will cause tragedy to come their way. They oppose themselves.

Remember: *Satan gets his power through deception.* God's people are destroyed for lack of knowledge.

Body of Authority

Jesus said:

Upon this rock I will build my church; and the gates of hell shall not prevail against it.

And I will give unto thee the keys of the kingdom of heaven: and whatsoever thou shalt bind on earth shall be bound in heaven: and what-

soever thou shalt loose on earth shall be loosed in heaven.

Matthew 16:18,19

The Amplified Bible says it differently: "I will give you the keys of the kingdom of heaven, and whatever you bind — that is, declare to be improper and unlawful — on earth must be already bound in heaven; and whatever you loose on earth — declare lawful — must be already loosed in heaven" (v. 19).

Just stop and ask yourself: What is bound out of heaven?

Sickness, disease, poverty — all that is evil.

Jesus Himself said you have authority to bind evil from the earth. You are not binding it from the whole earth; but you can bind it from the part you are walking on. However, you cannot bind it if you do not know you have the authority to do so.

As a believer, you need to realize that your body gives you authority on the earth. A spirit being must have a body in order to manifest himself in the earth.

That is why *satan has no legal authority here*. He does not have a physical body.

That is also why he hates your body and why he wants you sick, crippled, or dead.

When you lose your body, you lose your authority on earth — lose your right to operate here. Have you noticed that when people lose their bodies, they don't hang around long? The dead don't pray or bind the devil, and *the dead don't praise God!*

Satan has no authority on earth because he does not have a physical body. He had to borrow the body of a serpent to talk to Eve in the Garden. Deception is how he gets the authority to bring disaster.

Jesus said whatever you have authority to bind on earth has already been bound in heaven. **If you do not bind it on your part of the earth, it will not be bound!**

You can pray intensely for God to bind it, but He has done all He is going to do about it. Jesus said, *All power is given unto me in heaven and in earth. Go ye therefore, and teach all nations . . .* (Matt. 28:18,19).

What did He do with that power?

He delegated it to men. All power and authority of earth has been given to men. Jesus turned to His disciples and said, *Go ye into all the world and preach the gospel to every creature . . . In my name shall they cast out devils . . .* (Mark 16:15,17).

He said to men: "**You** go do it! **You** take the **power of My name** with the **authority of your body** and **you** do it!"

That corresponds with what He said to Peter: "I will give you the keys of the kingdom. Whatever you bind on earth is already bound in heaven. Whatever you loose on earth is already loosed in heaven." (Matt. 16:19.)

Do It Now!

Begin now to bind out of your life the things that have already been bound out of heaven.

Bind evil from your property! Bind it out of your home!

Jesus said, *The thief cometh not, but for to steal, and to kill, and to destroy* (John 10:10). If you give satan a free hand, that is exactly what he will do.

You can sit around and be religious if you want. You can say religious things like, "Lord, if it be Your will, heal me." But that will not get the attention of God. You have to know the will of God.

You must **know** it is God's will for you to walk in health.

You must **know** it is God's will that it be on earth as it is in heaven.

You must gain this knowledge if you are to enter into God's best.

Paul said in 2 Timothy 2:26, . . . *that they may recover themselves out of the snare of the devil.* He did not say somebody else was going to pray the prayer of faith and recover you out of the snare of the devil. It is an act of **your will** to recover **yourself** out of the devil's snare.

Tragedy after tragedy comes to Christians because of a lack of knowledge or because they fail to apply the knowledge they have.

Be a doer of the Word. **Being a hearer and not a doer of God's Word will allow tragedy to come to your house.**

The righteous is delivered out of trouble, and the wicked cometh in his stead.

Proverbs 11:8

5

The Right Foundation

In the sixth chapter of Luke, verses 46-49, Jesus talks about laying the right foundation. He describes two men: one is a success in life, the other is a failure.

And why call ye me, Lord, Lord, and do not the things which I say?

Whosoever cometh to me, and heareth my sayings, and doeth them, I will shew you to whom he is like:

He is like a man which built an house, and digged deep, and laid the foundation on a rock: and when the flood arose, the stream beat vehemently upon that house, and could not shake it: for it was founded upon a rock.

But he that heareth, and doeth not, is like a man that without a foundation built a house upon the earth; against which the stream did beat vehemently and immediately it fell; and the ruin of that house was great.

Notice in these two situations, both men heard the Word, but only one man stood against the stream. Some think that only one was saved, but that is not what Jesus said. Both men *heard* the Word, but only one was a *doer* of what Jesus said.

The person that only hears the Word says, "Glory to God! Isn't that good? Isn't that wonderful what the Word said!"

Then he walks on and allows destruction to sweep away his house. Disaster comes and he can only stand and watch, helpless. He has no power with which to stand against the storm.

You must act to resist the devil.

I ask you: What caused one house to fall and the other house to stand? (Of course, we know Jesus is not talking about a housing project, but men's lives.) What caused one man to perish and the flood to be disastrous to him?

It was the *same* flood, the *same* stream, the *same* storm that beat upon both lives. One could not be shaken, but the other one fell immediately. Notice Jesus did not say the house was not shaken; He said it was impossible to shake it.

The foundation made the difference!

The house that stood against the storm was built on a solid foundation and the foundation was laid on the solid Word of God. The foundation was *doing the sayings of Jesus*.

Jesus said, "I give you the keys of the kingdom. Whatever you bind will be bound; whatever you loose will be loosed."

I have heard people loose all kinds of things against their families. Full Gospel people stand in churches and give testimonies that are supposed to glorify God. They tell how satan is destroying their homes and causing all kinds of problems. Without knowing it, they are loosing the devil in behalf of their homes.

The things that come to your house are not necessarily what God wills, but what you allow. **God will allow anything you will allow.** It is not His responsibility to keep it out; it is **your** responsibility!

Maybe you have accepted tragedy as God's will so that you will learn from it, or so that other people will see good come from it. That, my friend, is satan's **number one** deception!

He deceives you into believing that the tragedy or problem you face is God's will. You reason: *If God is doing it, who am I to come against God?*

That kind of thinking will neutralize your faith. It stops your ability to operate in the realm of faith.

Build on the Word

Being a doer of the Word will build a foundation that satan cannot destroy — no matter how hard he tries!

Remember what Jesus did when satan came to Him on the Mount of Temptation: He spoke three words that built a firm foundation that satan absolutely could not shake.

To each temptation that satan brought, Jesus responded, *It is written!* Then He quoted what was written in the Scriptures.

His words shook satan's kingdom beyond repair. He has never been able to get it back together — and he never will!

By doing the same thing that Jesus did, you will get the same results. No matter how bad situations get, just say what Jesus says. Thank God, it brings deliverance!

Always remember: It was not *the storm* that caused the house to be destroyed; it was a lack of foundation. The man was not doing what Jesus said to do.

As a believer, you should be occupying and controlling the earth until Jesus returns. It is your place to hold fast and watch!

It is time that you operate in the principles of God's Word and walk in the ways God has designed for you. It will not work as long as you walk in the ways of the world.

You must do the sayings of Jesus if you are going to stand and not be shaken. You must speak to the mountain *because Jesus said to do so*.

Know God's Will

One of the most subtle attacks against the faith of any Christian is for satan to convince you that the situation coming your way is the will of God for you.

I have heard this lie preached all over the nation — from pulpits, on television, and radio. *Satan wants you to believe that everything coming to you in this life is the will of God for you.* But that is not true!

I asked this question of one minister who believed that way: "What about the guy who shot himself? Was that God's will for him?"

He answered, "Ultimately, it must have been God's will."

"Wait a minute! If it *was* God's will, what about Adam? God told Adam not to eat of the fruit of the tree of blessing and calamity. Was it the will of God for Adam to eat it when God had already told him not to do it?"

The minister replied, "You see, there is a revealed will of God and there is a secret will of God. That was God's revealed will for Adam not to eat; but secretly, it was God's will for Adam to sin so that He could send His Son to redeem mankind."

No wonder the world is confused — the Church is confused!

Thank God, it was **not** God's will for Adam to sin! It could not have been: God told him not to do it.

Someone may say, "Yes, but God *allowed* it."

They will say, "I know God didn't make me sick, but He *allowed* it."

Did God allow it?

What do you mean when you say that God allowed it?

Again, I refer to Jesus' words: "I give you the keys of the kingdom. Whatever you bind is bound; whatever you loose is loosed."

Who allowed it? You did!

The problem is we do not want to take the responsibility.

Jerry Savelle and I were conducting a seminar and were teaching that God has given us authority to use Jesus' name to stop these things. A man stood up and walked out of the meeting.

He said, "I can't accept that. You are putting all the blame on us!"

He wanted to put the blame on God!

If God lived on earth today and was guilty of doing only one-tenth of the things people have accused Him of doing, all His life on earth would be spent in prison. Wicked men would put Him there because, if He did what He has been accused of doing, He would be more wicked than they. Even wicked men pass laws to put away people who do things God has been blamed for.

Don't go back into the Old Testament and drag into the New Testament all that happened under that Old Covenant. **We are under a new covenant.**

That is why the Jews could not understand Jesus. He spoke of a loving heavenly Father, and they saw their God as a God of wrath.

The people in Old Testament times were under the Law. God's Word had been spoken. He said, "Don't do it. Don't get out there where the curses are; it will produce tragedy."

But they walked out there anyway, and the curses hit them — and God was blamed for it, even though he told them not to go where the curses were.

I realize the *King James Version* says in effect that God put all of these things on them, but you have to study the Hebrew to find the true meaning. It was written in an "allowing" sense rather than a "causing" sense.

Essentially, these things were not God's responsibility. God said it would be "thus and so" if they did that. God's Word was out; His law was established. When they did these things, they caused them to come to pass. Their disobedience caused the curse to come on them.

If they had not done it, would it have happened? No.

Then whose responsibility was it? It was not God's responsibility at all!

Do you see how people have charged God with things He was not responsible for? He just told them what the consequences would be.

Faith and Patience

My brethren, count it all joy when ye fall into divers temptations;

Knowing this, that the trying of your faith worketh patience.

But let patience have her perfect work, that ye may be perfect and entire, wanting nothing.

James 1:2-4

Throughout the New Testament, the Greek word for *temptations* is translated "trials and tests."

Notice it says, *when ye fall into divers temptations*. It is accidental when you *fall* into temptation. You are not deliberately walking into it.

However, I have seen many good Christians walk into things with their eyes wide open. Then they make remarks like:

"You know, God works in mysterious ways His wonders to perform. We don't understand it now; but we will, by and by."

"You never know what God is going to do."

"You know, the Bible says that all things work together for good."

If you read God's Word, you will know what He is going to do. God's ways are established. He always does what He said He would do in His Word. He will do all you will believe Him to do.

Many people experience tragedy because they believe the tests and trials coming their way are from God. They believe He sends trials to perfect them and cause them to mature, so they say, "Who am I to fight against God?" Then they bow down under it and allow the devil to steal everything they have.

But James 1:3 says nothing about trials *perfecting* and *maturing your faith*. He says the trying of your faith works *patience*. Then in verse 4, he says:

> But let patience have her perfect work, that ye may be perfect and entire, wanting nothing.

The Bible says that through *faith* and *patience* you possess the promises.

Patience is a spiritual force. It does not mean that you are to sit down and allow things to come. It means to be constant, unchangeable.

A long bridge must have piers of support so that it will not sag or fold when weight is applied. **Patience is a spiritual force that undergirds your**

faith, causing it to be constant throughout the trial or test that you fall into.

Actually, you have no *problems;* they are only *opportunities* to prove that God's Word works. Satan puts them there to destroy you. He designed them to bring calamity to your house.

Many people turn back into sin and give up when they are under trials and tests. If God were a part of that, He would then be partner to those people being lost.

These things are a design of the devil, not to perfect your faith, but to destroy you.

If you will operate in faith and allow patience to come and have its perfect work, then you will be perfect and entire, wanting nothing. Why? Because you acted on God's Word. It was simply an opportunity to prove that God's Word works.

Once you realize this and get a taste of victory, you will have no more desire for defeat.

When you are faced with tests and trials, you need to go to God for some answers.   James 1:5 says:

If any of you lack wisdom, let him ask of God, that giveth to all men liberally, and upbraideth not; and it shall be given him.

If you want to know the answer to a problem, ask God. I challenge you to ask Him. Go to His Word; the answers are there. God will not say anything to you that is different from what His Word says.

An individual stated in a certain pamphlet that he had asked God why his wife was suffering such sickness and why she had so many problems. He stated that the Lord said it pleased Him to bruise her.

He heard the devil.   That came straight from the pit!

Many are deceived by religious spirits. Certainly, they love God, but they are deceived. Isaiah 53:4,10 says it pleased God to bruise *Jesus!* He has

already borne the bruises so that we
would not have to bear them.

Satan pulled a scripture verse out of
context and convinced the man that his
wife's sickness was the work of God.
Through lack of knowledge, you can
invite tragedy.

> *Let no man say when he is
> tempted, I am tempted of God: for
> God cannot be tempted with evil,
> neither tempteth he any man:*

> *But every man is tempted, when
> he is drawn away of his own lust,
> and enticed. Then when lust hath
> conceived, it bringeth forth sin: and
> sin, when it is finished, bringeth
> forth death.*

> *Do not err, my beloved brethren.*

> *Every good gift and every perfect
> gift is from above, and cometh
> down from the Father of lights, with
> whom is no variableness, neither
> shadow of turning.*

James 1:13-17

When you are faced with a situation,
stop and ask yourself: *Is this good? Is*

it perfect? The answers to these questions will label it.

Then go back to John 10:10 — *the balance wheel of the Bible* — where Jesus says, *The thief cometh not, but for to steal, and to kill, and to destroy: I am come that they might have life, and that they might have it more abundantly.*

The Bible says in 1 John 1:5, *God is light, and in him is no darkness at all.*

Sickness and disease could not come from heaven because there is none there!

Calamity, problems, and troubles could not come from heaven; heaven has none! These things are bound out of heaven.

Again, I refer to Jesus' words: Whatever you bind on earth is already bound out of heaven. **You have the authority to do it.**

Be A Doer

>*But be ye doers of the word, and not hearers only, deceiving your own selves.*
>
>*For if any be a hearer of the word, and not a doer, he is like unto a man beholding his natural face in a glass:*
>
>*For he beholdeth himself, and goeth his way, and straightway forgetteth what manner of man he was.*
>
>James 1:22-24

Do you know what glass James is talking about? The mirror of God's Word. As you look into the mirror of God's Word, you can see these truths:

You are born of the Spirit of God.

You have the Greater One in you.

You have the world-overcoming faith of God inside you.

You have authority to use the name of Jesus and walk in victory.

Look at yourself in the mirror of God's Word; then turn and walk away.

If you are not a doer of the Word, you will forget what manner of man you saw in the Word. Then you will probably say, "I guess it's just God's will that these things come my way."

But whoso looketh into the perfect law of liberty, and continueth therein, he being not a forgetful hearer, but a doer of the work, this man shall be blessed in his deed.

James 1:25

The blessing of the Lord, it maketh rich, and he addeth no sorrow with it.

Proverbs 10:22

6

Wrong Thinking
and
Wrong Speaking

There is no doubt that problems come to everyone in this life. All of us face troubles, tests, trials, and opportunities to enter into calamity.

But God's will is that we resist these problems by the power of His Word — the word of deliverance.

God's will is that His angels deliver us. Psalm 91:11,12 tells us that He gives His angels charge over us: *They shall bear thee up in their hands, lest thou dash thy foot against a stone.*

If this is God's will, then why do so many Christians experience such defeat?

There are three links in the chain of defeat: **wrong thinking, wrong speaking, wrong praying.**

Wrong Thinking

You are what you are, not because of your experiences in life, but because of what you *think* and *believe* about your experiences.

Many Christians feel sorry for themselves and are wallowing in self-pity. They think God is against them, when actually the devil is doing it and blaming it on God! That kind of thinking leaves the door wide open to the devil.

So many Christians use what happened to Job as their excuse. They say, "But look what God did to Job!"

What *did* God do to Job? He gave Job twice what he had before.

It was **the devil** that stole from Job, **not God**. It was **the devil** that caused all the problems, **not God**.

Job made 74 false accusations against God because he really believed God was at fault. But Job could not read the first chapter of the Book of Job and find out that the devil was behind all his problems.

Here are some of the statements Job made about God:

Though God slay me, yet will I trust him. It was admirable that Job felt this way, but he was wrong in his thinking. God was not the problem.

He taketh me by the nap of the neck and shaketh me . . . He runs up on me like a giant. No, that was not God; it was the devil.

He sets darkness in my path. God did not set darkness in Job's path; but Job thought He did. Job was sincere, but he was sincerely wrong!

Two factors caused Job more problems than the actual troubles he had: *wrong thinking* and *wrong believing*.

Many precious people are crippled for life because of their wrong thinking. It cripples their ability to function in the wisdom of God and flow in the Spirit of God.

There is no darkness in God, so He could not have put darkness before Job. The Bible says that God is light and in him is no darkness at all. Every good and perfect gift comes down from above — from the Father of lights, with whom there is no variableness, neither shadow of turning.

Right and Wrong Choices

When you **think** wrong, you **believe** wrong. When you **believe** wrong, you **speak** and **act** wrong. **Wrong thinking** causes you to make **wrong choices.**

The reason there is so much wrong thinking in the earth today is because people do not know what God has said. Deliverance from these things only comes about through the knowledge of God and of His Word.

When people believe tragedy is working good in their lives, that problems and troubles are really making them stronger, they are opening the door to the devil. They are allowing satan to have a party at their expense. They will not stand against it because they believe it is from God; so they just let the devil run all over them. Then God gets the blame for all of it!

The deception of the devil is designed to destroy you by making you believe it is God's will that these things

happen to you. This is why the doctrine of praising God for everything that happens to you is so dangerous. It actually opens the door to the devil.

I am sure that God does not appreciate being thanked and praised for putting cancer on someone.

Satan's greatest tool is deception. If he can deceive you into believing whatever comes to you is from God, you will not resist it.

For instance, I heard of one man who had a supernatural visitation which he believed to be an angelic being. The being, which was glistening and arrayed in white, told him that his sickness was from God and that he would die with it. The man believed those words. He swallowed it — hook, line, and sinker!

Even though a prophet of God was sent to minister to him and bring healing to him, he would not accept it. He said, "No, the Lord told me that I am going to die and it is not His will to heal me."

If that man had known the Word of God, he would have known the visitation was *not* of God. Evidently, it was an angel of the devil. Paul said that the devil himself is transformed into an angel of light. (2 Cor. 11:14.)

Many people are deceived by supernatural visitations. Everything supernatural is *not* of God. Compare all that is said by any supernatural being with what the Word of God has to say.

If this man had known the truth, he would not have accepted that message. He did not have to die. He died needlessly and his family suffered needless tragedy because he believed the lie of the devil.

Many good Christians are deceived and think satan is perfecting the saints. God did not send the devil to perfect the saints. The Holy Spirit and the Word of God are perfectly capable of doing that. Ephesians, chapter 4, tells us that the five-fold ministry (apostles, prophets, evangelists, pastors and teachers) was provided by God for the perfecting of the saints.

If God were using sickness, disease, troubles, problems, car wrecks, and tragedies to perfect the saints, then when a member of the five-fold ministry comes to town for a meeting, his advertisement should read something like this:

Brother So-and-so is coming to town! As an apostle of God, he will give some car wrecks, some cancer, some lung disease, and some marriage problems for the perfecting of the saints.

That sounds ridiculous, I know, but it is no more ridiculous than to believe God is using the devil to perfect the saints. God is *not* using the devil! He is using the five-fold ministry, equipped with the Holy Spirit and the power of God's Word!

What does the five-fold ministry use to perfect the saints?

The Word of God.

Jesus said, *Now ye are clean through the word which I have spoken unto you* (John 15:3). Paul said that we are cleansed with the washing of water by the Word. (Eph. 5:26.)

Wrong Speaking

Let me again make this statement: When you **think** wrong, you **believe** wrong. When you **believe** wrong, you **speak** and **act** wrong.

Words produce images inside you. By your words, you can produce a failure image or a success image. Many have produced an image of tragedy in their hearts by their wrong speaking.

I share the following story, not to confuse anyone or put them down, but to help a multitude of people lest they follow the same pattern of fear. (I hesitate to share some of these things in this book, but I must do so. If I do not, many will fall into the same trap.)

A friend, who was scheduled for open-heart surgery, decided to read about the operation in a medical book. That was the worst thing he could have done! It produced fear.

The doctor told him: "We have had twelve of these operations in this hospital and all have been successful.

There is no reason to think this one won't be.''

But my friend said, ''Doctor, when you put my heart back in and hook it up, you will never get it started again.''

''Oh, yes, we will,'' the doctor said. ''You don't know what you are talking about. There is no reason to believe that it won't.''

I prayed with the man before surgery and led him in the sinner's prayer, so he would know he was ready to go. He was full of fear. He had already seen death, believed it, and embraced it.

He died on the operating table.

Your words establish the cornerstones of your life — or your death. Life and death are in the power of the tongue. (Prov. 18:21.)

A lady who had planned a trip overseas for a certain date made this statement:

''I told my husband three months ago, 'You just watch and see! The day we get ready to go, our children will be sick.' Well, today's the day, and they're sick!''

Isn't that amazing! She was snared by the words of her mouth. She invited trouble and then looked forward to it for three months. She seemed proud that she had "prophesied" it ahead of time.

In both of these situations, the person's words painted an image of failure and defeat. That is so often the case. People are defeated in life because **images of failure have been painted in their hearts by the words of their mouths.**

We must *unlearn some things* if we are to possess the promises of God. Israel failed to enter the Promised Land because they saw defeat — in spite of what God had said.

The Word of God in the New Testament is *our* "promised land." But we must possess it by faith. **We cannot go by experience.** We cannot go by what happened to a fellow Christian. **We must go by what God's Word says.**

Evil Words Defile

A man's very heart can be defiled by his words.

Jesus said in Matthew 15:11, *(It is) not that which goeth into the mouth, (that) defileth a man; but that which cometh out of the mouth, this defileth a man.*

In other words, it is not what you *eat* that defiles you; it is what you *say*. **Your words produce images for good or evil.**

Evil does not originate in the heart; it originates in the thought pattern. Evil is first a thought that is meditated and dwelt upon until it is conceived in the heart. Finally, you give birth to that thought by speaking it.

You cannot keep the devil from putting bad thoughts or doubts in your mind; but you can stop them there. *They will die unborn if you don't dwell on them or speak them.* The words you speak will produce (give birth to) the very images that are inside you.

> *But those things which proceed out of the mouth come forth from the heart; and they defile the man.*
>
> *For out of the heart proceed evil thoughts, murders, adulteries, fornications, thefts, false witness, blasphemies;*
>
> *These are the things which defile a man.*

Matthew 15:18-20

These images begin with the thought process. Then through meditation, they become infused in the heart. Once in the heart, **they will come out the mouth** for out of the abundance of the heart, the mouth speaks. All these things proceed from the heart.

Needless suffering comes to many because they have never learned these truths.

Let me share with you how to produce good images and get rid of unwanted images.

Paul says, . . . *Casting down imaginations and every high thing that exalteth itself against the knowledge of*

God (2 Cor. 10:5). You can do that, or Paul would not have said for you to do it.

Right now, I want you to picture a dog in your mind. You may be visualizing your dog, or perhaps your neighbor's dog. Let's say it is a black dog.

If I say, "brown dog," then you get a different image.

Now, start thinking about a cat — a white cat.

What happened to the image of the dog? It disappeared. You painted another image with words.

The word "breakfast" to one person may mean two boiled eggs. To someone else, it means poached eggs, or maybe scrambled eggs. Others may see Raisin Bran.

Words paint images. Let's say you are thinking about a car. If I start talking about an airplane, the image of the car disappears and is replaced by the image of an airplane.

This is how you cast down imaginations. When bad imaginations come up in your thinking, **change those images with your words by quoting and thinking God's Word.**

Paul put it this way: *Be not overcome of evil, but overcome evil with good.* Take the good thought, the good image, and fill your mind and heart with that. When you do, the bad images will disappear.

You can produce the images you desire by your own words and your own thoughts.

God set before Israel both blessing and cursing, but He told them to choose the blessing:

> *For this commandment which I command thee this day, it is not hidden from thee, neither is it far off.*
>
> *It is not in heaven, that thou shouldest say, Who shall go up for us to heaven, and bring it unto us, that we may hear it, and do it?*

Neither is it beyond the sea, that thou shouldest say, Who shall go over the sea for us, and bring it unto us, that we may hear it, and do it?

But the word is very nigh unto thee, in thy mouth, and in thy heart, that thou mayest do it.

See, I have set before thee, this day, life and good, and death and evil.

I call heaven and earth to record this day against you, that I have set before you life and death, blessing and cursing: therefore choose life, that both thou and thy seed may live.

Deuteronomy 30:11-15,19

In previous chapters, God has told Israel all the blessings and cursings of the Law. Then in the passage of Scripture set out above, He says, *See, I have set before thee this day, life and good, and death and evil.*

Notice how these are grouped together: first, *life and good*; then, *death and evil*.

I have set before you life and death, blessing and cursing: therefore choose life, that both thou and thy seed may live.

The choice is yours — a choice similar to what Adam was faced with in the Garden of Eden. You can choose life and good, **or** you can choose death and evil. You can choose blessing, **or** you can choose cursing.

No one can make that choice for you. It is one you must make yourself.

But God has made a way of escape from the evil. With any temptation that comes your way, God will always make a way of escape that you may be able to bear it. God does not bring the trouble, but **He will make a way of escape.**

Verse 20 says, *Love the Lord thy God . . . for he is thy life, and the length of thy days: that thou mayest dwell in the land which the Lord sware unto thy fathers, to Abraham, to Isaac, and to Jacob, to give them.*

You may say, "Yes, but that promise was to the children of Israel."

No, this is a promise to God's people. It is a promise for you today — **if** you will believe it and receive it. God said, *I call heaven and earth to record this day.*

Let's say, as an example, that you have been diagnosed as having cancer and the doctors say you must die. You have a choice:

Life and Good **or** Death and Evil

Blessing **or** Cursing

Christ has redeemed you from the curse of the Law so that the blessing of Abraham might come upon you. The doctors have only told you what they know medically.

Begin now to choose life. **God has set before you life and death, blessing and cursing; therefore, choose life.**

You don't have to die of cancer! You don't have to spend the rest of your life in a wheelchair. You don't have to bow down to calamity and problems and troubles. Take the name of Jesus and break the power of that thing over your body.

Some families have a history of sickness and disease. Is this true of your family?

Have you ever said, "I'll probably die young"?

If you have, then begin to say, "No, I refuse that! I renounce those words. In the name of Jesus, I'll change my confession." By doing so, you can change your destiny.

You have the authority to choose. No one else can make the choice for you.

According to Proverbs 18:21, *Life and death are in the power of the tongue.*

Some people have been taught that miracles are not for today, that we are to accept whatever comes to us; but that is a lie of the devil!

Yes, miracles *are* for today. **If you want a miracle to come to your house, begin to choose life instead of death;**

good instead of evil; blessing instead of cursing.

Believe God for the best. Believe Him for a full life. Believe the best of every situation that you are facing. Don't allow tragedy to come into your life.

Jesus has given you the keys of the kingdom. Whatever you bind on earth will be bound in heaven; God will back whatever you bind. Whatever you loose on earth is loosed in heaven; God will see that what you loose is loosed. **Don't loose death; loose life and health.**

If ye be willing and obedient, ye shall eat the good of the land. But if ye refuse and rebel, ye shall be devoured . . . (Is. 1:19,20). The children of Israel walked in disobedience and received a just recompense of reward. They never obtained the Promised Land, even though it was theirs.

If you believe the lies of the devil, you will **never** possess what belongs to you. **God has given you life and blessing.** He has given unto you all things that pertain unto life and godli-

ness. But to enjoy that kind of life and godliness requires the knowledge of God.

If the doctor has said you have cancer and you are going to die, God's Word and your voice can change that. Speak forth what God has said:

By whose stripes ye were healed (1 Pet. 2:24); and, *With his stripes, we are healed* (Is. 53:5).

He bore **your** iniquities. He carried **your** diseases. He suffered pain and agony for **you**.

Begin to agree with this and say what God said. You *can* come off your deathbed. You *can* be healed. The cancer growth *can* be destroyed, for you are delivered from the powers of darkness. **But you must choose.**

Choose life! Don't choose death.

Life is for you *today*. A miracle is for you *today*.

Don't invite tragedy by the words of your own mouth — by agreeing with the devil, by agreeing with all that is bad and evil. You can change it with *your words* and *God's Word*.

God will change your life. He will change your situation, **if** you will agree with Him.

You don't have to give up life. You don't have to give up because **Jesus is the same yesterday, today, and forever: the Healer!**

The thief comes only to steal, kill, and destroy; but Jesus said, "I am come that you might have life and have it more abundantly."

Don't choose death; **choose life!**

Don't choose sickness; **choose health!**

He shall call upon me, and I will answer him: I will be with him in trouble; I will deliver him, and honour him.

With long life will I satisfy him, and shew him my salvation.

Psalm 91:15,16

7

Wrong Praying

Prayer is one of the prime areas satan uses to bring disaster to Christian homes. This does not mean we should quit praying; but we must learn to pray *accurately* and *effectively*.

Wrong praying brings defeat.

I have read of many people who were crippled for life after they prayed a prayer such as, "Oh, God, whatever it takes, just bring me to the place I ought to be."

That is an open invitation to the devil. Every bad thing, every calamitous thing, that comes will be accepted as being from God.

Many dear Christians have suffered needless tragedy because of their wrong praying.

For instance, they pray, "God, I am willing to suffer whatever it takes to bring me to a closer walk with You."

That is what I call an "open-ended prayer." It leaves an opening for satan to slip in and bring troubles, even tragedy.

If you are willing to obey God, He will lead you. He will give you direction by His Spirit and His Word. He will cause the Word to work in your heart and change your desires.

He will bring you to the place He wants you to be *without* breaking your legs or causing you to be a cripple for the rest of your life.

All God wants you to do is be obedient to the direction of His Word.

The Holy Spirit and the Word of God are perfectly capable of getting you to that place; He does not need the devil's help!

Pray the desired results. Pray for the leading of the Holy Spirit. Pray to be perfected by the Word.

But prayer alone will not change a situation. You must bring the words of your mouth under control.

Prayer for healing is almost useless if you are going to confess sickness and disease day in and day out!

Prayer for prosperity will go unnoticed if you continually confess that no good deals ever come your way and you never have enough.

Your words will cancel your prayers.

Wrong praying destroys faith.

The Bible says that the prayer of faith shall save the sick and the Lord shall raise him up. (James 5:15.) This being true, then there must be an opposite principle, since there are two opposing forces in the earth — the Spirit of God and the spirit of the devil.

If the *prayer of faith* will *save* the sick, then the *prayer of doubt* will *destroy* the sick. (I know this is a strong statement, but it is true.)

Wrong praying can destroy you. Prayer releases spiritual forces. When prayed accurately according to the Word of God, the forces of God will become activated in your life. But a prayer that is filled with doubt, fear, and unbelief will activate the evil forces of the enemy in your life.

In Mark 11:23, Jesus set forth a principle:

> *For verily I say unto you, That whosoever shall say unto this mountain, Be thou removed, and be thou cast into the sea; and shall not doubt in his heart, but shall believe that those things which he saith shall come to pass; he shall have whatsoever he saith.*

Jesus did not say it would come to pass at that very moment; He said, *He shall have whatsoever he saith.*

This is a *spiritual* principle — not a prayer scripture, but a *faith principle.* We could call it *the law of faith.*

Jesus begins the next verse with the word *therefore,* which means "because of the preceding verse." A man shall have what he says; *therefore, it will work in prayer.*

> *Therefore I say unto you, What things soever ye desire, when ye*

pray, believe that ye receive them, and ye shall have them.

What *them* is He talking about? *Them* things you prayed! (I realize this is not good grammar, but it will help you understand this verse.)

Let me paraphrase this scripture: The law of faith says a man will have what he says if he doubts not in his heart, but believes those things which he says will come to pass. Therefore, this law will work when you are praying.

If you pray the *problem*, it will grow greater and things will get worse. If you pray the *answer*, you are releasing the answer, and the problem will be solved.

In essence, Jesus is saying you will have what you say, *even in prayer*. All satan has to do is twist your vocabulary and get you to pray the problem:

"Lord, the money is not coming in. We're going to lose our home. What are we going to do? Lord, we will never get out of debt!"

Let me show you the principle behind this. Your words are going into your spirit and your spirit man is receiving it. **God's Word is His will toward man. Man's words should be his will toward God.**

Jesus said, *But let your communication be, Yea, yea; Nay, nay; for whatsoever is more than these cometh of evil* (Matt. 5:37).

He is saying: Speak what you desire — the thing you *want* — to come to pass. Don't speak what you are *afraid* will come to pass. *Satan has deceived the Body of Christ into praying their fear rather than their faith.*

Faith and Fear — Opposite Forces

Let me share with you a parallel of these forces.

Hebrews 11:1 says, *Now faith is the substance of things hoped for, the evidence of things not seen.*

Faith is the substance — the raw material — of the things you hoped for. It is the substance of things desired.

Fear is an exact opposite to faith. It is diametrically opposed to faith.

Faith comes by hearing *the Word of God*.

Fear comes by hearing *the word of the devil*.

If *faith is the substance* of things desired, then *fear is the substance* of things not desired. Both fear and faith will cause things to come to pass. Fear is the reverse gear of faith, the evil part of the tree of blessing and calamity.

Many people wonder why God allowed things to be set in the earth this way. God had nothing to do with it! He set the tree in the Garden and gave Adam a choice. Then He gave him all the information needed to make the right choice; but Adam *chose* calamity. When he did, he lost control of his tongue. His words worked against him.

Fear is produced by hearing and meditating on words of the devil.

Fear is the force that produces the very thing you do not desire. You must resist it like you would resist the devil.

If you don't, it will bring tragedy to your home.

You can stop fear with the name of Jesus and the Word of God in your mouth. Say to fear: "I rebuke you and command you to leave, in Jesus' name."

Satan Steals Health

As I have traveled throughout the United States teaching in seminars, I have heard wrong praying in more than one place. The Lord began to show me prayer patterns where tragedy has struck.

I remember hearing the testimony of a pro-ball player who testified that before going into a certain bowl game, he prayed, "Lord, I'll love You just as much whether I come out of this game hurt or well."

Of course, we should love God the same no matter what our condition is; but we are not required to pray that way. The Bible says we are to *pray the thing we desire.*

The end result for that man was needless suffering. He came out of the game with a pulled muscle in his leg, which left him crippled for several months. He did not know he was praying wrong and his lack of understanding opened the door to the devil. *The thief cometh not, but for to steal, and to kill, and to destroy* (John 10:10).

Never pray, "Lord, I'm willing to give my life if my family would just get saved." You will be issuing a special invitation for the devil to bring tragedy to your home. *You are not required to pray that way*.

Satan Steals Life

One dear sister in a certain city gave this testimony before 1,000 people: She had a desire to know God in a greater way, so she prayed, "Dear Lord, I'll give up everything but my husband to get closer to You."

It is admirable that she was willing to do that, but she did not know what the Word said. It was not necessary for her to give up anything except sin!

Her prayer did not bring the results she wanted, so she prayed again: "Lord, I am even willing to give up my husband to know You better."

Now, let's judge this prayer by the Word.

Paul said, *Neither give place to the devil* (Eph. 4:27). This woman's lack of knowledge opened the door to satan. She was willing to give up everything she owned, including her husband, if she could only get closer to God.

Although her willingness to sacrifice is to be admired, it is *totally unscriptural*. What she actually did, without realizing it, was offer a human sacrifice — her husband!

Within three months, her husband was dead.

When you make this kind of "deal" with God, you are actually trying to offer *another sacrifice* that will save your family or bring you closer to God.

But **Jesus was the only sacrifice** that had to be offered! He has already died for you and for your family.

You are not required to offer your life on the altar of sacrifice for a loved one. That is idolatry. Certainly, the Bible says you are to offer your body as a sacrifice to God; but it says to offer it as a *living* sacrifice, *not a dead one!*

After her husband's death, she testified that God took him and it brought her closer to God. **Lack of knowledge brought needless suffering.**

Paul said, *That they may recover themselves out of the snare of the devil.* The devil walked into that situation and said, "This is the perfect set-up. Anything we do to her husband will be received by her as being from God."

I am not belittling the individual; she had not been taught the truth. There are multitudes of people who are doing the same thing. They don't know, but they need to know! That is the only reason I have shared this incident.

Jesus was the only sacrifice that had to be offered to bring us closer to God.

The devil walked in and destroyed God's creation. That person could not use her faith because she believed the trouble was from God. Without knowing it, she was inviting tragedy by her prayers.

That is the reason for this book: to educate people to the tricks of the devil. Many people today are praying, "Lord, whatever it takes, let it come."

You need to know the truth. The knowledge of the truth will set you free!

Satan Steals Finances

In another city, there was a couple who owned a good business and had no lack in the financial realm.

The woman was born again and filled with the Spirit. She loved God with all her heart, but her husband was unsaved.

She prayed, "Lord, whatever it takes, I want my husband saved. Lord, I'll give up anything. I am willing to give up everything we own if my husband would be saved."

It is admirable that anyone would be willing to do that, but you are not required to do it. Besides, it is idolatry. She was trying to trade their finances for her husband's salvation. You don't make deals like that with God. There is only *one way:* through Jesus.

She made the sacrifice. Some months later, the business started to decline. It went down, down, down. They lost everything they owned and were absolutely wiped out — in bankruptcy.

She proclaimed: "God answered my prayer. My husband turned to God."

It is great that her husband turned to God, but he could have been saved and still kept his business.

Let's analyze this prayer on the basis of scripture. "Whatsoever things *you desire* when you pray, *believe that you receive them and you shall have them.*"

She could have prayed:

"Father, in the name of Jesus, send laborers across my husband's path and minister the Word of God to him.

"I charge the angels and the ministering spirits to see that the right people come across his path.

"I stand upon the Word of God in the name of Jesus and I believe he is saved and filled with the Holy Ghost.

"In Jesus' name, I'll not be moved by what I see, feel, or hear. I see him saved through the eye of my faith."

. . . *all things, whatsoever ye shall ask in prayer, believing, ye shall receive* (Matt. 21:22).

Who Is The Thief?

Did God answer that woman's prayers? Did He steal their finances and use it as a sacrifice or bribe to get her husband saved?

No! She invited the devil into their finances. The devil is the thief and he came to steal and to destroy.

If she had pulled out the "Bible measuring stick" and stood it beside that prayer, she would have seen who was behind it.

God is **not** out to steal your finances and your loved ones. **The devil is!**

Death is **not** of God, and never has been. **Death is of the devil!** The Bible says death is the last enemy that will be destroyed. It is an enemy of God and man.

Don't open the door to the devil. Don't invite tragedy into your home by praying foolish prayers, inspired out of self-pity and defeat. The Word gives you principles to go by. If you apply those principles, your husband or wife or children will be saved without needless loss.

Many people believe that troubles and heartache lead to repentance, but Romans 2:4 tells us: *The goodness of God leadeth thee to repentance.*

Pray Your Desire

In a prayer meeting where I was teaching several years ago, one dear sister decided to pray her desire. After I had finished teaching on confessing the Word, she stood up and said, "I want to pray."

I said, "Go right ahead."

Here is what she prayed: "Thank You, Father, in the name of Jesus, that my husband is saved and filled with the Holy Ghost, that we have a Christian home and our children love the Lord."

She prayed her every desire.

One lady leaned over to her and said, "I didn't know your husband was saved."

I said, "See, it's already working! You already have one person agreeing with you!"

About a year later, I was back in that prayer group. The woman's husband had received Jesus as Lord and was there that day! When I gave an invitation for those that wanted to receive the baptism of the Holy Spirit, her husband came forward and received.

That woman held fast to her confession of God's Word. She prayed the answer instead of the problem. She learned the secret of effective praying:

If you pray the problem, you will have whatever you say, even in prayer.

Do you know why that is so?

Because the heart of man produces either faith or fear, depending on what you feed into it. You will begin to believe what you pray. If you pray the problem, you will believe the problem more than you believe the answer.

Some people say, "Oh, you're just ignoring the problem."

Oh, no! I am doing what Jesus said to do: I am praying the answer.

Jesus said to pray *whatsoever you desire.*

One lady stood up in church and said, "Pray for my husband. I have been praying for him for twenty-five years! But he's getting meaner. He won't go to church with me."

The devil had conned her into praying what already existed. It was true that he was not saved, that he was mean, that he would not go to church; but that was the *problem,* not the *answer.*

She needed prayer more than her husband. He *knew* he was wrong. She thought she was pleasing God with that doubt and unbelief, but instead she was violating every principle of faith and prayer.

The Spirit of God spoke into my spirit: "She's been praying the problem all these years. If she had prayed the answer, her husband would have been saved more than twenty years ago — but she has held fast to the problem."

Her prayers held him in bondage!

Stop Foolish Prayers

You may have prayed some prayers which opened the door to satan and have already seen some manifestations of it. You can stop the foolish things you have said in prayer.

Right now, I want you to pray a prayer which will nullify those foolish things:

Father, in the name of Jesus, the entrance of Your Word has brought light to me. Because Your Word has said it, I believe it; and from this hour forth, I will pray my desires. I will rebuke the problem, speak to it, and tell it to be gone!

Father, I repent of all the foolish prayers I have prayed, of all the things I have set into motion which would work against me. With the authority of my words, I break the power of every foolish word which I have spoken, in Jesus' name.

No evil will befall me. Neither shall any plague come nigh my dwelling. You have given Your angels charge over me. They keep me in all my ways. In my pathway is life and there is no death.

I am a doer of the Word of God.

I am blessed in my deeds.

In Jesus' name, I stop every force that has been set in motion by my foolish words.

I ask Your forgiveness and I receive that forgiveness now. I will keep my mouth and speak only that which edifies. I will let no corrupt communication proceed from my mouth in prayer or in speech. I will speak only that which is good for edifying, that it will minister grace to the hearer. I will not grieve the Holy Spirit of God.

Now, Father, in Jesus' name, I proclaim that I am delivered from the powers of darkness. I am standing in the liberty of the Lord Jesus Christ and walking in victory, for the Greater One dwelleth in me.

In Jesus' name, it is so!

8

Your Heart Produces
What You Plant

If any man among you seem to be religious, and bridleth not his tongue, but deceiveth his own heart, this man's religion is vain.

James 1:26

This is a strong scripture. There are many people who *seem* to be religious; but because they do not bridle their tongues, satan does not have to deceive them. **They deceive their own hearts by the words they speak.** They say things foolishly and speak things which they do not desire to come to pass.

As I was staying in the home of a friend, he walked past me, carrying a trash bag over his shoulder. He jokingly said, "Well, I finally came to my calling in life — carrying out the trash."

He walked about two steps and said, "No, wait a minute. I bind those words in Jesus' name!"

Of course, just because he said it once does not mean he would become a trash collector; but if he continues to say things like that, it would get into his heart.

It Starts in the Mouth

Jesus had much to say about the words we speak. It all centers around **the law of faith — Mark 11:23:**

> *For verily I say unto you, That whosoever shall say unto this mountain, Be thou removed, and be thou cast into the sea; and shall not doubt in his heart, but shall believe that those things which he saith shall come to pass; he shall have whatsoever he saith.*

Eventually, it will come to pass.

We know this statement is true because Jesus said it. But not many people understand it. Some would say, "Those people who are making those faith statements are lying."

But Jesus said:

Out of the abundance of the heart the mouth speaketh. A good man out of the good treasure of the heart bringeth forth good things.

Matthew 12:34,35

Who brings it forth? **The man.**

Where does he bring it from? **His heart.**

How? Out of the abundance of the heart, **the mouth speaks.**

What you receive in your heart will get into your mouth; and what you have in your mouth will get into your heart. **It starts in the mouth!** Paul said, *But what saith it? The word is nigh thee, even in thy mouth, and in thy heart* (Rom. 10:8).

First, it is in your mouth; *then,* it gets in your heart. But once in the heart, it gets back in the mouth.

Foolish things people say get into their hearts and *deceive their hearts.*

The spirit of man is designed to lead and guide him. The Holy Spirit abides in the human spirit. The *human spirit* is a design of God; it was breathed out of the mouth of God.

Notice Genesis 2:7:

And the Lord God formed man of the dust of the ground, and breathed into his nostrils the breath of life; and man became a living soul.

It was the breath of God — the Spirit of God — which became the spirit of man, the human spirit. It was an exact duplication of God's kind. God is a spirit and man is a spirit. Man has a soul and he lives in a body.

Man's spirit is designed to communicate with God. Paul asked, *What man knoweth the things of a man, save the spirit of man which is in him? even so the things of God knoweth no man, but the Spirit of God* (1 Cor. 2:11).

If the Spirit of God knows all about God and your human spirit knows all about you, then when your spirit contacts God's Spirit, you have tapped the Source of all knowledge. This is what you do through the baptism in the Holy

Spirit. Your spirit is fellowshipping with Deity.

Although every born-again human spirit can contact God, there is a greater avenue of flow between you and God when you have the prayer language of the Holy Spirit. *He that speaketh in an unknown tongue speaketh not unto men, but unto God* (1 Cor. 14:2).

Your born-again spirit is in contact with God; therefore, it will search the avenues of God's wisdom to find answers to the things fed into it by your words.

Your words determine what answer your spirit seeks for. When you under-stand that, you will know why Jesus said:

Every idle word that men shall speak, they shall give account thereof in the day of judgment.

For by thy words thou shalt be justified, and by thy words thou shalt be condemned.

Matthew 12:36,37

The word *idle* means "non-working." Jesus said you will give an account on the day of judgment for any word you speak that is not working for you. Why? Because it is fed directly into your heart.

Proverbs 16:9 says, *A man's heart deviseth his way*. The way you go when you get up tomorrow is devised by your human spirit.

Your spirit is guided by the words you speak and by the information it gains from the knowledge of God.

Remember: The kingdom of God is the domain of God. Jesus said, *The kingdom of God is within you*. **The dominion God has in you is in your human spirit.**

With the understanding, then, that our human spirits lead and guide us, let's find out how God works through this kingdom.

Your Heart Is The Soil

Jesus told a parable of the sower. He said, *The sower soweth the word* (Mark 4:14).

In this parable, He speaks of four types of soil. When you get His interpretation, you find that *the soil* represents *the heart of man* and *the seed* represents *the Word of God.*

You sow the Word in your heart.

Paul said the Word is first in your mouth, then in your heart. **When it gets into your heart, your human spirit works night and day to find a way for it to come to pass.**

Here is an example: There is a thermostat on the wall of your home. The thermostat is the goal setter of your furnace and air conditioner. When you turn the dial to 70 degrees, the heart of that unit will work day and night until it brings the house to that temperature.

That unit is designed to produce whatever temperature is set on the thermostat.

The spirit of man is what the Bible calls "the heart of man." (Gen. 45:26,27; Rom. 2:29.) The spirit is designed to operate in the God kind of faith.

The human spirit is the production center. Whatever a man feeds into his spirit is what the unit (spirit) will work to produce. The heart of man will work night and day to produce what he "dials" in it (by his words), the same as the thermostat (the heart of that unit) will work to bring the temperature to that setting.

The heart of the unit does not say, "Wait a minute! I think you need cold air instead of hot." It cannot think. It does not have the ability to think. The unit is only designed to produce what you dial into the thermostat.

The inner man (your spirit) will lead you **according to what you have fed into it** — whether good, bad, or indifferent. The spirit of man devises his ways. Keep your heart with all diligence for out of it are the forces of life. (Prov. 4:23.) This is where it all comes from.

Good or evil comes from the inside of man.

> *But those things which proceed out of the mouth come forth from the heart; and they defile the man.*

> *For out of the heart proceed evil thoughts, murders, adulteries, fornications, thefts, false witness, blasphemies.*

Matthew 15:18,19

Led or Misled

Your spirit will guide you into a position to cause what you are saying to come to pass. This may explain why you have been misled at times. You have deceived your heart with words.

Your spirit worked night and day to bring you into a position to cause to come to pass things you really did not want.

But you spoke wrong words into your spirit day in and day out. You prayed wrong words. You *prayed* the problem. Your heart received that as being your will and worked day and night to bring you into a position where the things you were saying would come to pass.

You might have said, "Well, I know that God led me into that business deal."

Well, maybe *your spirit* led you. There is a fine line here. Yes, God does lead you through your spirit, **but you programmed the wrong information into your spirit.** It is not what goes into the mouth that defiles a man, *but that which cometh out of the mouth* (Matt. 15:11).

Your spirit works day and night to gather information from God, Who is the Source of all knowledge.

If you have confessed or prayed defeat, your spirit asks, "What must he do to fail? What will it take to get him into a position where he will go bankrupt? What will it take to get him into a position where his car will fall apart before it is paid off?"

The human spirit has access to this kind of information. What man knows the things of man but the spirit of man?

Heart Soil

> *And these are they which are sown among thorns; such as hear the word,*
>
> *And the cares of this world, and the deceitfulness of riches, and the lusts of other things entering in, choke the word, and it becometh unfruitful.*
>
> *And these are they which are sown on good ground; such as hear the word, and receive it, and bring forth fruit, some thirtyfold, some sixty, and some an hundred.*

Mark 4:18-20

Now notice: **Only one type of soil brought forth fruit** — the soil that received the seed. In other words, it was prepared. It did not have thorns or stones in it.

We must pull out some thorns and throw out some stones that would be stumbling blocks, for they keep the Word of God from taking root. Jesus made this statement: *Satan cometh immediately, and taketh away the word that was sown in their hearts* (v. 15).

The Seed You Sow Are Words

We have determined that the sower is sowing words; and Jesus said these words are sown in the heart. So *the soil* Jesus is talking about in Mark, chapter 4, is *the heart of man,* or the human spirit. That is where you sow the Word of God.

Paul said in Romans, chapter 10: *Faith cometh by hearing, and hearing by the word of God . . . the word is nigh thee, even in thy mouth, and in thy heart.*

The sower sows the Word. You are the sower. You are sowing seed. Every day, out of your mouth, you are sowing either God's Word or the devil's word!

According to the Law of Genesis, *everything produces after its own kind.*

If you speak faith-filled words, your words will produce faith in your heart.

If you speak fear-filled words, those words will produce more fear. When you talk about a recession and repeat all the bad news, you will feed fear into your heart.

You can transmit either faith or fear by the words you speak.

The Word says that you sow words into the heart. Your heart is the soil that will produce the fruit. Sowing God's Word (speaking in agreement with God's Word) puts it into your heart.

Fruit Is Produced

The human spirit will produce anything that is planted in it.

The sower sows the Word, and the heart is the soil in which that Word is sown.

Jesus gives another parable in Mark 4:26,27:

And he said, So is the kingdom of God, as if a man should cast seed into the ground;

And should sleep, and rise night and day, and the seed should spring and grow up, he knoweth not how.

Man has no idea how this works!

Perhaps you have been led into a situation and you don't know how you got there, or why God led you there. You may have deceived your own heart, and your spirit led you there. Then you thought it was God leading you because it came from within you. But you were deceived.

You deceived your own heart by wrong speaking, wrong thinking, and wrong praying.

For the earth bringeth forth fruit of herself (v. 28). What is the *earth?* Jesus has already established that the earth (soil) is the heart or spirit of man. It is designed to bring forth what is planted in it.

If a farmer plants cotton, cotton will grow. If he plants soybeans, soybeans will grow.

A farmer decides what the ground will produce by the seed he plants. The soil is not designed to think. It will raise cucumbers, apples, marijuana, poppies, anything that is planted. The soil will never decide whether or not it is right or wrong to produce a particular plant. *The seed determines the product.*

For the earth bringeth forth fruit of herself. So does the human spirit.

The spirit will produce whatever is planted in it. The heart of man was designed to produce good; but by planting the wrong seed, you can make it bring forth evil.

Jeremiah said, *The heart is deceitful above all things, and desperately wicked: who can know it!* (Jer. 17:9). He found it would produce whatever was put into it. As a man that was not born again, he considered the heart to be evil.

Jesus made the comparison of the heart and the soil. Soil is not evil; it is basically good. Though it can be used for evil — to grow dope, poison, or thorns — the soil itself is not evil. The evil is in the seed which is sown. The Law of Genesis says *the seed is in itself.* The enemy sowed the bad seed.

The heart will bring forth **evil** or it will bring forth **good**. **The output is a result of the input.** The born-again human spirit will have a **bad output** if it has the **wrong input.** Being the right-eousness of God (as far as known sin in concerned) does not mean you cannot speak evil seed into your heart.

You can be right in your heart, but wrong in your head; and your head will deceive your heart.

James said the *heart* is the *governor of the tongue.* Your spirit accepts your words as being your will. Wrong words sown in the human spirit long enough will get you on the railroad track when the 9:23 comes along! **Your human spirit will lead you to what you confess — good, bad, or indifferent.**

When you realize the power of the Word of God and confess it over finances, your spirit will work overtime, finding ways to bring to pass what you say. Sometimes it takes weeks and months to get the Word of God in the soil of your heart.

People, who do not understand this principle of confessing God's Word, get very upset when they see others prospering by confessing the Word.

They say, "I don't understand why their income doubled three times this year, while mine went down. No good deal ever comes my way. Every time I get a good job, I lose it."

With their words, they are programming their human spirits to defeat and failure.

Suppose you make this statement: "If anybody gets laid off at the plant, I'll be the first one." By speaking this over and over, you will eventually deceive your heart.

Your human spirit will act on those words and search the avenues of God's wisdom to find out how you can be the first to be laid off. A run-in with the boss or a long disagreement will do it.

Some day you will feel led to be very disagreeable with the plant manager, and what happens? You are the first one laid off. Then you say, "Why did God allow this to happen?"

God had nothing to do with it. The words you spoke deceived your heart. You planted the wrong seed, and your heart worked day and night to bring that seed into production.

Remember, Jesus said, *Out of the abundance of the heart, the mouth speaketh.*

Whatever is abundantly in your heart will come out your mouth. That is why you can be around people for only a few minutes and locate whether they are operating in faith or fear. It will come out their mouths.

The governor of the tongue is the spirit, or heart. If you deceive your heart, you will be talking the problems.

> **And the tongue is a fire, a world of iniquity: so is the tongue among our members, that it defileth the whole body, and setteth on fire the course of nature; and it is set on fire of hell.**
>
> James 3:6

The word *course* is translated from a Greek word that means " a circuit of physical effects." In other words, the tongue will set about a circuit of physical effects in the body.

Did you ever hear someone sneeze and say, "I believe I'm taking the flu. I believe I'm coming down with something"?

Every time a symptom hits your body, the first thing you want to do is tell somebody. You say, "My neck aches; and you know, that's the first symptom of the flu. I'm coming down with it sure as the world."

Before long, you have talked yourself into it. Every defense system of your body will stop and let it come. When you describe the symptoms to people, they will agree with you: "Yep, that's just the way the flu starts!" And Jesus said, *If any two of you agree . . .* (Matt. 18:19).

Several years ago, I decided that if I could have what I said, I would start saying something else. So, when I sneezed, I began to say, "Thank God, I'm taking healing!"

One day a lady said to me, "I thought you were already healed."

"I am, but I'm storing it up!"

Your words will cause a circuit of physical effects. God cannot be "out-talked." Whatever way a man speaks, that same way will he also walk.

What you say is truly what you will get.

A certain fellow went fishing with me; and before we reached the lake, he started saying, "I know I'm not going to catch any fish today. I know you'll catch them all. I never catch any."

And he didn't!

He deceived his heart. *His spirit took his words to be his will.*

Let me give you an illustration of what happens in a situation like this.

The man begins by saying what he expects, based upon past experience. He continues to say what he cannot have. Then he goes fishing and throws his line up a tree or hangs it on a log. He says, "Every time I get a good place, I hang up. I never can get in where the fish are."

So, he continually throws his line where there are no fish.

He says, "There's a good place!" But he throws the plug where there never have been any bass. His spirit led him, but his spirit had not been fed the right words.

Because he is always saying, "I'm not going to catch any fish," his spirit leads him to places where he will not catch anything.

Not only does it work this way while fishing, but in every area of your life.

Your words are programming you either to failure or to success.

> *The tongue of the wise useth knowledge aright: but the mouth of fools poureth out foolishness.*
>
> Proverbs 15:2

> *A man shall eat good by the fruit of his mouth.*
>
> Proverbs 13:2

9

Strife — An Open Door to Satan

Out of the same mouth proceedeth blessing and cursing. My brethren, these things ought not so to be.

Doth a fountain send forth at the same place sweet water and bitter? Can the fig tree, my brethren, bear olive berries? either a vine, figs? so can no fountain both yield salt water and fresh.

Who is a wise man and endued with knowledge among you? let him shew out of a good conversation his works with meekness of wisdom.

But if ye have bitter envying and strife in your hearts, glory not, and lie not against the truth. This wisdom descendeth not from above, but is earthly, sensual, devilish. For where envying and strife is, there is confusion and every evil work.

James 3:10-16

Here again, we find the importance of the words we speak. James lists **two more reasons why tragedy comes into the lives of many.**

> *If any man among you seem to be religious, and bridleth not his tongue, but deceiveth his own heart, that man's religion is vain.*
>
> James 1:26

A person can pray the best prayer ever; but **if he does not control his tongue, he can destroy that prayer with only a few words.** Words of envy and strife can set confusion in motion and cause more problems than he can get out of in three weeks!

When the problems come, he cries out to God: "Oh, God, why in the world did this come to pass? God, why did You allow it?"

But God had nothing to do with it. That man violated the laws of God.

Let me give you an example from personal experience.

My wife Peggy and I were coming from a teaching seminar in New York and were flying on a commercial flight.

The man in charge instructed the passengers to board according to the color of their passes; so we stood there, being obedient to his instructions. However, the other passengers ran on, trying to board first since there were no assigned seats. It was first come, first served! We were the last ones to board, of course, so we had to take the seats that were available.

We had been up late traveling and were tired; and Peggy got a little upset over it. I didn't appreciate it either, but she got into strife and became very negative about it. (She didn't say anything bad, but she did get into strife.)

Then, she could not find our tickets. She had the ticket to board the plane, but the others were gone. She searched her purse, looked everywhere! She thought she had lost them.

We called the stewardess and had her phone back to see if we had left them at the airport when we boarded the plane. We spent 30-45 minutes trying to get tickets to replace those that were lost.

After a while, Peggy found the tickets. They were in her coat pocket all the time!

Where there is strife, there is confusion and every evil work.

Christians let satan into their lives through strife. Paul said we are to give him *no place*. **We** are in charge. **We** can keep satan out or give him a place to work. **Don't give him any place!**

Let not the sun go down upon your wrath (Eph. 4:26).

One minister friend said, "Many times I have had to break the speed limit to get home before the sun went down to tell my wife, 'Honey, you were wrong, but I forgive you anyway!'"

Don't let the sun go down on your wrath. Why? Because where there is strife, there is confusion and every evil work.

Strife in the home is an open door to satan. If not corrected, it will bring tragedy to your marriage and to your home.

Again, a new commandment I write unto you, which thing is true in him and in you: because the darkness is past, and the true light now shineth.

He that saith he is in the light, and hateth his brother, is in darkness even until now.

He that loveth his brother abideth in the light, and there is none occasion of stumbling in him.
1 John 2:8-10

These verses were written by the Apostle John, who lived to be an old man in a day when it was not popular to believe what he believed.

Tradition tells us that he was boiled in oil, but he refused to die. They sent him to the Isle of Patmos to get rid of him. Then he wrote the book of Revelation!

He lived through all the persecution, and it would be wise for us to listen to what he had to say.

He that loveth his brother abideth in the light, and there is none occasion of stumbling in him.

But he that hateth his brother is in darkness, and walketh in darkness, and knoweth not whither he goeth, because that darkness hath blinded his eyes.

1 John 2:10,11

There are many Christians who start out in love, but end up in strife with their brother. They open the door wide to the devil.

We just read a profound truth: "If you walk in the light, there is no occasion of stumbling; but he that hates his brother is *in darkness* and *does not know where he is going.*"

It may seem that everything is going right, but the Word says that man does not know where he is going. He will stumble and not know what he is stumbling over.

*We know that we have passed
from death unto life, because we
love the brethren. He that loveth
not his brother abideth in death.*

1 John 3:14

**Unforgiveness and strife cause
tragedy in Christian families. Anyone
living in unforgiveness or strife is
abiding in death.**

Paul said, *For the law of the Spirit
of life in Christ Jesus hath made me
free from the law of sin and death*
(Rom. 8:2).

If you walk in love and fellowship
with Jesus, you are walking under the
law of the *Spirit of life.*

If you hate your brother, you abide
under the law of the spirit of death.

*Whosoever believeth that Jesus
is the Christ is born of God: and
every one that loveth him that begat
loveth him also that is begotten of
him.*

*By this we know that we love the
children of God, when we love God,
and keep his commandments. For*

this is the love of God, that we keep his commandments: and his commandments are not grievous.

1 John 5:1-3

John wrote, *For this is the love of God,* not the *love of man.* We get God's love and man's love mixed up sometimes. *This is the love of God, that we keep his commandments.*

Do you always feel like keeping God's commandments?

Do you always get up in the morning and feel like going to work? No. You know it is the thing to do, so you make a decision to do it.

We are told that the love of God is keeping His commandments. This is a **decision** we must make, not a **feeling.**

This is where many Christians get confused. They think, "I just can't feel right toward that individual." When you make the decision to walk in love toward that person, *your feelings will change.*

That is like saying to the fireplace, "Send me some heat and I'll put in some wood." It doesn't work that way!

When you decide to walk in love, your feelings will change; but until you make that decision, it will not work for you.

For whatsoever is born of God overcometh the world: and this is the victory that overcometh the world, even our faith.

Who is he that overcometh the world, but he that believeth that Jesus is the Son of God?

1 John 5:4,5

You can operate in this love because faith works by love. Our faith is the victory that overcomes the world!

This is why the faith of some does nothing for them. They are not walking in love. They get upset and "lose their cool."

When you are not walking in love, your faith is ineffective.

Love is something you **decide** to do.

Make the decision to walk in love right now!

And we have known and believed the love that God hath to us. God is love; and he that dwelleth in love dwelleth in God, and God in him.

Herein is our love made perfect, that we may have boldness in the day of judgment: because as he is, so are we in this world.

1 John 4:16,17

Are you having trouble with fear? If you are, then check to see if you are walking in love. John said:

There is no fear in love, but perfect love casteth out fear: because fear hath torment. He that feareth is not made perfect in love.

We love him, because he first loved us.

If a man say, I love God, and hateth his brother, he is a liar: for he that loveth not his brother whom he hath seen, how can he love God whom he hath not seen?

1 John 4:18-20

This is one of the most powerful passages in the Bible. It ties God with the creation of man. God created man in His own image and likeness — an exact duplication of kind.

Man is a spirit; he has a soul; he lives in a body. God is a Spirit. John writes that if a man says he loves God and hates his brother, he is a liar. If he does not love his brother whom he has seen, how can he love God whom he has not seen?

Both God and man are spirit beings. John said if you do not love the one, you cannot love the other because they are an exact duplication of kind. Jesus said, "If you have seen Me, you have seen the Father." He was the image of God.

"Do you mean Christians are walking in death?"

Yes! John said, *He that loveth not his brother abideth in death.*

This does not mean you are eternally lost. It means you are walking under the law of sin and death; and that law will be working on you. It can even cost you your life. If you are abiding under that law, you have given the devil a place in your life.

A Decision

Beloved, let us love one another: for love is of God; and every one that loveth is born of God, and knoweth God.

1 John 4:7

God is love. If you are born of God, you are born of love.

You may say, "But I just can't love that person."

Love is not something you always feel like doing. The love that John is talking about is the love of God.

Do you think God felt like giving His Son for the ungodly?

Do you think God had to have a certain feeling to give His Son?

No. He did not feel like it. He **decided** to do it! **Love is a decision, not a feeling.**

How can you love God if you are not going to love the creation which is created in the image of God?

Keep in mind, I did not say you would *feel* the same way about them as you do about your best friend; but you *decide* to love the unlovely. This is God's love.

Fight Fire with Fire

God's love is the decision to walk in love.

That is one of the hardest things I have ever done. Almost every time I went into a restaurant, I would get into strife. The thing that bothered me most was the waitress. She would be there every time I turned around *until* I wanted the check. Then, where was she? Gone, disappeared, vanished! We would sit there for twenty minutes trying to get our check!

I would get upset and tell my wife, "I'm not going to leave her a tip."

Then one day the Spirit of God said to me, "Why don't you fight fire with fire? The devil is just trying to get you upset."

So I *decided* to walk in love. (I certainly didn't feel like it; but I decided to do it anyway.)

The next time that happened in a restaurant, I told my wife, "I *was* going to leave a dollar tip, but now I'm going to leave her *two* dollars!"

Though a waitress may be late with the coffee, or bring the wrong order, or forget half of it, make the decision to walk in love. Whether or not you feel like it, do it anyway.

Make that decision, for love is of God! Give no place to the devil!

My son, keep my words, and lay up my commandments with thee.

Keep my commandments, and live; and my law as the apple of thine eye.

Proverbs 7:1,2

10

Unforgiveness, A Thief

Then came Peter to him, and said, Lord, how oft shall my brother sin against me, and I forgive him? till seven times?

Jesus saith unto him, I say not unto thee, Until seven times: but, Until seventy times seven.

Matthew 18:21,22

Certainly, you will not feel like forgiving your brother that many times; but by deciding to walk in love, you will be walking in God's love, not man's love.

Jesus continued by telling His disciples a parable:

Therefore is the kingdom of heaven likened unto a certain king, which would take account of his servants.

And when he had begun to reckon, one was brought unto him, which owed him ten thousand talents (about ten million dollars!)

> *But forasmuch as he had not to pay, his lord commanded him to be sold, and his wife, and children, and all that he had, and payment to be made.*
>
> *The servant therefore fell down, and worshipped him, saying, Lord, have patience with me, and I will pay thee all.*
>
> *Then the lord of that servant was moved with compassion, and loosed him, and forgave him the debt.*
>
> Matthew 18:23-27

Notice the phrase, *forgave him the debt.*

In that day, slaves were bought and sold. That servant and his family were about to be sold to pay the debt. But he pleaded for the king to have patience with him.

So the king said, "Okay, *I will forgive you all the debt!"*

> *But the same servant went out, and found one of his fellowservants, which owed him an hundred pence:*

(about $17) *and he laid hands on
him, and took him by the throat,
saying, Pay me that thou owest.*

Matthew 18:28

That servant had just been forgiven
of a $10 million debt, and here he is
choking a guy for $17! He has
received mercy, but is unwilling to have
mercy on his fellowservant.

*And his fellowservant fell down
at his feet, and besought him, saying, Have patience with me, and I
will pay thee all.*

*And he would not: but went and
cast him into prison, till he should
pay the debt.*

Matthew 18:29,30

He put his fellowservant under
confinement and condemnation. He
held that man in bondage and took
away his freedom for such a small debt.

*So when his fellowservants saw
what was done, they were very
sorry, and came and told unto their
lord all that was done.*

Then his lord, after that he had called him, said unto him, O thou wicked servant, I forgave thee all that debt, because thou desiredst me:

Shouldest not thou also have had compassion on thy fellowservant, even as I had pity on thee?

And his lord was wroth, and delivered him to the tormentors, till he should pay all that was due unto him.

Matthew 18:31-34

This sounds like a contradiction, but it is not. The king said, "I have forgiven you the debt." He established that fact twice; but then it states that he delivered the servant to the tormentors* till he could pay all that was due.

Is the king talking about the $10 million that the servant owed him? No. He can't be. He has already forgiven the servant of that debt. He can't charge him with that debt again.

---

*In those days, prisons employed men who were called "tormentors." These men used whips, embedded with glass and steel, to beat prisoners until they were willing to do whatever was required of them.

What then is he talking about? He is referring to the debt of forgiveness he himself has already received from the king.

Jesus closes the parable by saying:

So likewise shall my heavenly Father do also unto you, if ye from your hearts forgive not every one his brother their trespasses.

Matthew 18:35

Who is the tormentor today?

The devil.

In other words, Jesus said that **unforgiveness will put you in the hands, or power, of the devil.**

I am not saying that every tragedy occurs because an individual will not forgive; but unforgiveness is one of the major causes of tragedy. It will put you into satan's hands! It will open the door to the devil and you will be in the tormentor's hands until you forgive.

At a certain meeting several years ago, there was a lady who had a disease in her body which was causing her many problems. She said, "I'm going to be taught the Word of God; and one night, I will get in the healing line and receive my healing."

During one of the morning meetings, the minister taught on forgiveness and that unforgiveness keeps people from getting their healing and opens the door to the devil.

When the meeting was over, the lady called her brother that she had not spoken to in twenty years. She asked him to forgive her, and they settled their differences right then over the telephone.

That lady did not **feel** like doing it. She just made the **decision** to do it. **She decided to walk in love.**

She returned to the meeting that night; and before the healing line was formed, every symptom had left her body. She was healed!

Don't try to judge other people concerning this. Search your heart and apply it to your own life.

If you do not forgive, you will be turned over to the tormentor; and satan will have free access to your life.

Don't Stop Your Faith

And the Lord said, Simon, Simon, behold, Satan hath desired to have you, that he may sift you as wheat:

But I have prayed for thee, that thy faith fail not: and when thou art converted, strengthen thy brethren.

Luke 22:31,32

The Greek word translated *desire* can also be translated *demand*. Satan *demanded* to have Peter so he could sift him as wheat! Satan demanded that Peter be given into his hands so he could test and try him.

Now why did satan demand to have Peter?

There is some evidence in the Bible to indicate that Peter was impulsive and capable of getting into strife quickly! (If anyone needed peppermint-flavored shoes, Peter did. He was always getting his foot in his mouth!)

When the soldiers came to get Jesus, Peter pulled his sword and cut off a man's ear!

When you walk out of love into strife, you open the door to tragedy because strife will stop your faith.

Jesus said, "I have prayed for you that your faith fail not."

You see, your faith can fail to produce when you do not walk in love. **The law of faith never fails. It always works** because it is a law of God. **But you can fail to work it by not walking in love;** and you will invite tragedy into your life.

When you walk in unforgiveness, satan can *demand* to have you. He has God's Word for it. There is nothing God can do about it because He has already given His Word.

The penalty for walking out of love is too great. It can cause physical problems, financial problems, disaster of every form — and it is not God's will. It is a just recompense of reward from the devil.

Read Isaiah 38:1-5 and you will see how God sent Isaiah to Hezekiah to tell him: *Set thine house in order: for thou shalt die, and not live.* Hezekiah turned his face to the wall and repented. He did not change God; he changed himself and lined up with God's will for his life.

Before Isaiah could leave the building, God told him to go back and say, *I will add unto thy days fifteen years.* Not only did God give Hezekiah fifteen more years, He made the sun go back ten degrees on the sundial to prove that He was going to do it!

God will "bend over backwards" for you if you will operate in His law of love.

Many Christians die prematurely because they have not been obedient to God's Word. **Unforgiveness is truly a thief of life.** God said:

With long life will I satisfy him, and shew him my salvation.

Psalm 91:16

Yes, you can extend your life by operating in the principles of God's Word.

My son, forget not my law; but let thine heart keep my commandments:

For length of days, and long life, and peace, shall they add to thee.

Proverbs 3:1,2

Happy is the man that findeth wisdom, and the man that getteth understanding . . .

Length of days is in her right hand; and in her left hand riches and honour.

Proverbs 3:13,16

11

The Sin Unto Death

If any man see his brother sin a sin which is not unto death, he shall ask, and he shall give him life for them that sin not unto death. There is a sin unto death: I do not say that he shall pray for it.

1 John 5:16

This scripture does not say, "Don't pray for *the man*." It says, "Don't pray for *the sin*."

If you see a person who sins a sin not unto death, you can pray for that person and get condemnation off of him.

Do you know what condemnation does to an individual? It makes him run *from* God instead of to God. The devil is the one who brings condemnation. He wants you to think God is mad at you.

This scripture says you can pray for an individual and get that condemnation off of him so he will turn to

God. But if he sins *the sin unto death,* don't pray for that sin, because you cannot get that condemnation off of him.

I am convinced from studying the Scriptures that *the sin unto death* is unforgiveness. Let me show you why. We often quote Mark 11:23,24; but let's go two verses further:

> *And when ye stand praying, forgive, if ye have ought against any: that your Father also which is in heaven may forgive you your trespasses.*
>
> *But if ye do not forgive, neither will your Father which is in heaven forgive your trespasses* (vv. 25,26).

Jesus said the Father will not forgive you if you do not forgive others. He *will not* forgive you because He *cannot* — His Word is out.

The sin of unforgiveness is the most devastating sin any individual can get involved in. Why? Because it is *a continuing sin.*

You could get mad, sock a guy in the jaw, and say things you shouldn't. Then you could go to him and say, "Brother, I'm sorry. Forgive me. I shouldn't have done that."

When you ask the Lord to forgive you according to 1 John 1:9, it will be just as though it had never happened in the sight of God.

Sin, such as the one I described, is a one-time act.

Unforgiveness is not a one-time act, it is a continuing sin.

Let's say you have unforgiveness in your heart against someone, so you pray, "Lord, Your Word says if I confess my sins, You are faithful and just to forgive my sins and cleanse me from all unrighteousness. So forgive me, Father, of this sin."

Will God forgive you? No.

Why? Because you have not forgiven. You still have unforgiveness in your heart. You are trying to be forgiven for something that is a continuing act of sin. You are trying to get the Lord to forgive you for what you are doing, not just what you have done.

That unforgiveness will be a continuing act of sin until the day you die. Unless you forgive, God will not forgive you. Jesus said God will turn you over to the tormentors.

Refuse Strife

Again, let me emphasize the deadliness of strife. Tragedy after tragedy in Christian homes has come because the families are in strife.

I have known individuals who have come down with disease, even though they seemed to be standing on and confessing the Word of God. They were confessing the right things, but there was strife in their lives.

There was one such individual who took a strong stand on the Word of God. When that person died, many people questioned: "Why did that person die of that disease?" It seemed to them that they were strong in faith; but there was strife, bickering, and confusion in the home. It was absolute chaos at times.

It is no surprise that satan is able to bring sickness, and even premature death, to many because of strife and unforgiveness.

There was a certain lady that was diagnosed by the doctors as having tuberculosis. They told her to take the medicine prescribed, or she would have to go to a sanitorium.

Having heard some of the faith message, she made a stand: "No, I'm healed by the stripes of Jesus. I'm not going to take any medicine."

The doctors were going to place her in a sanitorium because they did not understand what she was saying. As far as they were concerned, she had tuberculosis.

She had just enough knowledge of faith to get her into trouble. She got into strife with her family. They wanted her to take the medicine, but she said, "No, I'm healed."

That *is* what the Word says, but the strife with her family stopped her faith. They were mad at her and she was mad at them. She was getting worse and the doctor wanted to put her in the sanitorium.

My wife Peggy felt impressed of the Spirit of God to go to her house and talk with her. As she did, the lady began to tell her the problem.

Peggy encouraged her to take the medicine. She said, "No medicine is going to heal you and no medicine is going to keep you from getting healed. But you are in strife; and where there is strife, there is confusion and every evil work.

"Take the medicine and, as you take it, say, 'Thank You, Father. I believe I receive my healing.' Right now, you are in strife and your faith is not working."

The lady said, "Maybe you're right."

She started taking the medicine; the family forgave one another; and everything was peaceful in the home.

Two weeks later she was asked to come in for x-rays. They x-rayed her once, then again. They called her in and, with much surprise, said that she had no sign of anything on her lungs. They had no idea why, but her lungs were totally clear. They said the medicine could not have cleared it up so fast. Faith works by love.

This woman could possibly have lost her life by getting into strife and unforgiveness. Sometimes it is better to compromise in love than to make a stand of faith in strife, for *faith worketh by love.*

He Is Just

God cannot forgive you of the sin of unforgiveness until you forgive.

Someone might ask, "But what about 1 John 1:9? It says if you confess your sins, He is faithful and just to forgive you and cleanse you from all unrighteousness."

Notice the Word says that He is faithful and *just!*

If God forgave you when you had unforgiveness in your heart, He would be *unjust* because of what Jesus said in Mark 11:26: *If you do not forgive, neither will your Father which is in heaven forgive you your trespasses.*

The Word of God is very plain to us about forgiveness. Many have had problems in this area.

Some are mad at God.

Some will not forgive themselves. **It is as important to forgive yourself as it is to forgive others.**

You can see that you *must* recover *yourself* out of the snare of the devil. Refuse to stay in the hands of the tormentor!

You do not have to walk that way any longer. The entrance of the Word brings light. **Now that light has come, recover yourself out of the snare of the enemy.**

God has already given His view:

*My people are destroyed for
lack of knowledge.*

Hosea 4:6

*But whoso hearkeneth unto me
shall dwell safely, and shall be quiet
from fear of evil.*

Proverbs 1:33

Charles Capps is a retired farmer who travels throughout the United States, teaching and preaching God's Word. He shares from practical, first-hand experience how Christians can apply the Word  to the circumstances of life and live victoriously. Besides authoring several books, Charles has a nationwide radio ministry and hosts a daily TV broadcast called "Concepts of Faith."

Charles and his wife Peggy make their home in England, Arkansas, and have two daughters: Annette, an ordained minister with offices in Tulsa, Oklahoma; and Beverly, who is currently studying for the ministry.

Other Books by Charles Capps

*The Tongue
A Creative Force*

*Releasing the Ability of God
Through Prayer*

Can Your Faith Fail?

*Changing the Seen
and
Shaping the Unseen*

*God's Creative Power
Will Work For You*

Authority in Three Worlds

For a free brochure of books and tapes by Charles Capps, write:

Charles Capps Ministries
Box 69
England, AR 72046